THE CITY of SARDIS

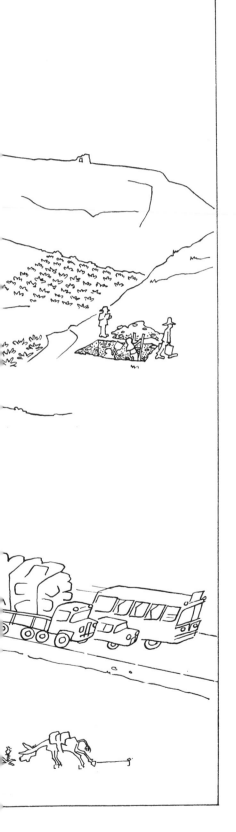

THE CITY of SARDIS
APPROACHES IN GRAPHIC RECORDING

Crawford H. Greenewalt, Jr.

Nicholas D. Cahill

Philip T. Stinson

Fikret K. Yegül

Harvard University Art Museums

Cambridge

Frontispiece. Drawing of excavation trenches at Sector MMS in the summer of 1978, with architects, excavators, and the local scene; view looking south.

Elizabeth G. Wahle, 1978, black ink on paper, 31.3 × 38.4 cm (12¼ × 15⅛ in.). Archaeological Exploration of Sardis, MMS-149.

This interpretive drawing was made for a Sardis *Newsletter*, to show then-current excavation at the site of the Lydian city wall, discovered two years previously. In the background is the Acropolis; at lower left part of the Synagogue forecourt. The low hill on the far side of the road (where two architects are operating a transit) is where remains of the city wall were first recognized (in the north scarp of the hill). Excavation in the shoulder of the road, where widening in about 1950 had removed part of the hill and "sectioned" the wall, has located the two sides of the wall, thereby establishing its width and north-south orientation; excavation at far right, middle ground, has exposed wall continuation to the south, and at lower left, in the dogleg trench, a gateway. At this time the hill itself was privately owned and under cultivation, therefore not available for excavation; it was later purchased by the Expedition. Excavated earth, including the unsightly heap in the foreground, was removed by a Citroën dump truck (given to the Expedition in 1959, still going strong in 2003); a Dumpster belonging to that truck appears on the road shoulder. The road is the highway connecting Ankara, the capital, with Izmir, the third largest city in Turkey. It is two-lane and two-way, and the traffic situation at far right is not exaggerated. The same landscape and view, in 1969, appear in fig. 3 (in the Introduction).

The City of Sardis: Approaches in Graphic Recording is the catalogue of an exhibition organized by the Archaeological Exploration of Sardis, Harvard University Art Museums, Cambridge, Massachusetts, on view August 23 to November 16, 2003.

This publication was funded by the Henry P. McIlhenny Fund in the Andrew W. Mellon Publication Funds, with additional funding from the Andrew W. Mellon Foundation, and from a gift in memory of Burriss Young, Helen Burriss Young, and Francis Hastings Young.

LIBRARY OF CONGRESS CATALOGING-IN-PUBLICATION DATA

The city of Sardis : approaches in graphic recording / Crawford H.
   Greenewalt, Jr. ... [et al.].
       p. cm.
   Includes bibliographical references and index.
   ISBN 1-891771-32-9
   1. Sardis (Extinct city)—Exhibitions——Catalogs. I. Greenewalt,
   Crawford H. (Crawford Hallock), 1937–
       DS156.S3C58 2003
       939'.22–dc21   2003010182

PRODUCED BY THE PUBLICATIONS DEPARTMENT
HARVARD UNIVERSITY ART MUSEUMS

Evelyn Rosenthal, Head of Publications
Edited by Joseph N. Newland, Q.E.D.
Production managed by Becky Hunt, assisted by Marcella Kligman
Designed by Christopher Kuntze
Cover artwork created by Nicholas D. Cahill
Printed by MacDonald & Evans, Braintree, Massachusetts

Illustration Credits

Archaeological Exploration of Sardis: cats. 1, 2, 10–14, 17, 24, 25, 41, 44, 46–50;
   figs. 16, 18, 23, 30–32, 34, 36
Nicholas D. Cahill: fig. 21
Elizabeth Gombosi: figs. 20, 24, 27, 29
Crawford H. Greenewalt, Jr.: figs. 2–5, 15, 19
Eliza Proctor: fig. 22
Christopher H. Roosevelt: fig. 1
Bonnie T. Solomon: figs. 25, 26
Luna Velazquez: fig. 35
Balloon aerial photograph by J.W. and E. Myers. Courtesy of the Archaeological
   Exploration of Sardis: fig. 28
Harvard University Art Museums, Department of Imaging and Visual Resources
   Katya Kallsen: Frontis; cats. 6–8, 15, 16, 18–23, 26–38, 40, 42, 43, 45;
       figs. 10, 17, 33
   Junius Beebe: cats. 9, 39
Reproduced by kind permission of the Joint Library of the Hellenic and Roman
   Societies, © Ken Walton: figs. 6–9, 12–14
V&A Picture Library: fig. 11
Yale Center for British Art, Richard Caspole: cats. 1, 3–5; fig. 15

Permissions:

The quote of Cyriacus of Ancona on p. 26 and in cat. 4 is reprinted by permission
   of the publishers from *Cyriac of Ancona: Later Travels*, edited and translated
   by Edward D. Bodnar with Clive Foss, The I Tatti Renaissance Library, 10,
   Cambridge, Mass.: Harvard University Press, Copyright © 2003 by the President
   and Fellows of Harvard College, Letter 6, cap. 4.
The Archaeological Exploration of Sardis wishes to thank Dr. Lenore Keene
   Congdon, Dr. Susan Heuck Allen, and Mr. Kendall F. Bacon for permission to
   quote the letter of Francis H. Bacon in cat. 8.
The Turkish contour maps discussed in cat. 45 were prepared at the request of the
   Archaeological Exploration of Sardis and transmitted through the Ministry of
   Culture, Republic of Turkey, by the General Command Headquarters of Maps
   (Harita Genel Komutanlığı).

Contents

Director's Foreword

As a specialist in old-master prints, I have always been fascinated by the systems of notation developed for specific printmaking techniques and functions. The most familiar is the "dot-and-lozenge" network perfected at the end of the sixteenth century in the Netherlands and used to this day for the engraved portraits on United States currency. This system (and countless others) has its special role in creating a graphic reality for a particular audience and purpose.

I have always thought my fascination with modes of graphic syntax a taste not shared, or even understood, in other disciplines, and so you can imagine how delighted I was to learn about the conceptual basis of this exhibition celebrating the Harvard-Cornell Archaeological Exploration of Sardis. I had assumed that it would be an exhibition of models, drawings, and photographs, which would inform our visitors about the discoveries at Sardis, and that is indeed what we have presented in the Fogg Museum's Straus Gallery. Yet, at the brilliant inspiration of Philip T. Stinson, one of the catalogue authors, it has been organized not by the date of ancient sites or structures, but by the date of discoveries and, more significantly, the means of their documentation.

It is self-evident that washy drawings by eighteenth-century gentlemen are not the same as twenty-first-century computer-generated overlays, even when they record the same site, but the differences are not simply a matter of knowledge accumulated over the intervening centuries. Our exhibition organizers have delved below the surface of technical change to discover significance in the mind-set and modalities of archaeological recording. What did these men (and, more recently, women) want to learn from the antiquities at Sardis? Does an architect recording an Ionic capital see differently, and thus select a different tool and style of drawing than an archaeologist might, or a conservator? What were the excavators of earlier years blind to? Does new technology transform vision? These are the questions that our exhibition organizers posed to themselves, and now pose to our museum visitors and the readers of this catalogue. Their questions and answers should resonate far beyond consideration of a single ancient site in distant Turkey.

My predecessor, James Cuno, proposed this exhibition, and I know that all of the exhibition's organizers join me in thanking him for his initiative and support, especially for his allocation of the Art Museums' Andrew W. Mellon Foundation Endowment through which we publish the catalogue. The Harvard University Art Museums are also deeply indebted to Crawford H. Greenewalt, Jr., and Elizabeth Gombosi, Field Director and Associate Director of the Archaeological Exploration of Sardis, who have brought exhibition and catalogue to such a successful realization. This would have been impossible, of course, without the contribution of our authors, Greenewalt and Stinson, together with Nicholas D. Cahill and Fikret K. Yegül. I thank them, just as they thank their predecessors, whose labors in the field, on paper, and now in electronic media, have brought us to a deeper understanding of the complex significance of the historical archaeological record.

Marjorie B. Cohn
Acting Director
Carl A. Weyerhaeuser Curator of Prints

Preface

In August 2001, James Cuno, Elizabeth and John Moors Cabot Director of the Harvard University Art Museums (1991–2002), generously invited the project called Archaeological Exploration of Sardis, or Sardis Expedition, to present an exhibition for the Art Museums and to prepare an exhibition catalogue. Originally scheduled for 2004, to be part of seventy-fifth anniversary celebrations for the Fogg Art Museum building and the conservation department (the fiftieth anniversary of the Sardis Expedition falls in 2008), the exhibition later was rescheduled for 2003, to coincide with the International Congress of Classical Archaeology, held in Boston that summer, and to replace an exhibition that required more time to prepare.

An exhibition of architectural and topographical drawings, which could be prepared in the time available and with minimal adjustment of Expedition commitments to fieldwork and publication, was suggested by Elizabeth Gombosi, Sardis Expedition Associate Director. Several important and little known drawings of the eighteenth and early nineteenth centuries were located nearby, in New Haven, at the Yale Center for British Art; and the Expedition possessed a large archive of drawings prepared over a period of nearly forty-five years. Those drawings, supplemented by others, could illustrate continuity and change in the aims and approaches of architectural and topographical recording over a period of two and a half centuries, and preparatory sketches could communicate the process of recording. Although none of the Expedition drawings had been made for museum display, many were of high quality and all illustrate landscapes and monuments of historical and cultural significance. Many of the drawings are published here for the first time; others have appeared only in professional journals.

The organization of the exhibition, around the concepts and headings called Brush Strokes, Crisp Lines, Dashed Lines, and Infinite Points, was conceived by Philip T. Stinson, and proposed by him in the summer of 2002. Stinson, who has been a recording architect at Sardis for twelve seasons and senior architect for nine of them, and Fikret

K. Yegül, who has studied two major ancient buildings of Sardis (the Roman Bath-Gymnasium Complex, which he published, and the Temple of Artemis, of which he is preparing an architectural study) are closely familiar with Sardis architecture and architectural history. Nicholas D. Cahill, who has excavated at Sardis since 1979, is well versed in Sardis topography and mapping (having supervised the digitization of maps prepared for the Expedition by the Turkish General Directorate of Maps, in Ankara, and Global Positioning System recording of site topography in 2001). Elizabeth P. Baughan supplied important information about the decoration of the painted tomb chamber at Lale Tepe. Elizabeth Gombosi (who has a long association with the Expedition, beginning with her years as staff photographer, 1968–77 and 1983), organized the exhibition and catalogue, corresponded with lending institutions, coordinated preparations at the Fogg Art Museum, and monitored the quality of photographic reproduction. Katherine Kiefer, Expedition Publications Editor, worked with the authors to prepare the catalogue manuscript for submission to the Harvard University Art Museums Publications Office, and made many perceptive suggestions regarding both style and content. The Director of the Manisa Museum, Hasan Dedeoğlu generously permitted and encouraged publication of the tomb chamber of Lale Tepe; he and his successor, Müyesser Tosunbaş facilitated access to the chamber for study and recording.

The Sardis Expedition is deeply grateful to James Cuno for his invitation to hold an exhibition in the Fogg Art Museum, for offering exhibition space in the Straus Gallery, for authorizing the underwriting of major catalogue costs from the Henry P. McIlhenny Fund in the Andrew W. Mellon Fund and the Andrew W. Mellon Foundation, and catalogue publication by the Harvard University Art Museums, and for continuous and enthusiastic encouragement; and to Marjorie B. Cohn, Acting Director of the Harvard University Art Museums in 2003, for her staunch and heartening support of exhibition and catalogue. Others at the Art Museums who contributed in major ways to exhibition and catalogue include Penley Knipe and Tony Sigel (Conservation), Danielle Hanrahan and her staff (Exhibitions), Rachel Vargas (Registrars Office), Andrew Gunther, Katya Kallsen, Junius Beebe III, and Julie Swiderski (Digital Imaging and Visual Resources), and Evelyn Rosenthal and Becky Hunt (Publications). The catalogue has benefited from the sound and tasteful ideas of Joseph N. Newland (editor) and Christopher Kuntze (designer).

The important loans of older graphics and a model from New Haven, Princeton, and New York that add historical, artistic, and physical dimension to the exhibition were authorized through the good will and generous efforts of: Amy Myers (Director), Elisabeth Fairman (Curator of Rare Books and Archives), Scott Wilcox (Curator of Prints and Drawings), Timothy Goodhue (Registrar), and Melissa Fournier (Assistant Registrar) at the Yale Center for British Art; Shari Kenfield (Curator of Research Photographs) and Christopher Moss (Editor of Publications) at the Department of Art and Archaeology, Princeton University; and Bonni-Dara Michaels (Collections Curator) at Yeshiva University, New York City. Pieter B. F. J. Broucke (Professor of the History of Art and Architecture) at Middlebury College alerted Sardis Expedition members to the existence of the drawing by C. R. Cockerell at Yale.

A portion of the catalogue costs were defrayed by a gift to the Sardis Expedition for its publication program, from the late W. C. Burriss Young, in memory of himself and of his parents, Helen Burriss Young and Francis Hastings Young. The Expedition is pleased and proud that Burriss Young and his parents are an intimate part of the catalogue. Costs of exhibition installation, loan shipments, conservation, and photography from lending institutions, as well as of preparing Sardis Expedition materials, were defrayed by a gift from an anonymous friend of the Sardis Expedition.

Deep and heartfelt thanks to each and all of the above.

Crawford H. Greenewalt, Jr.

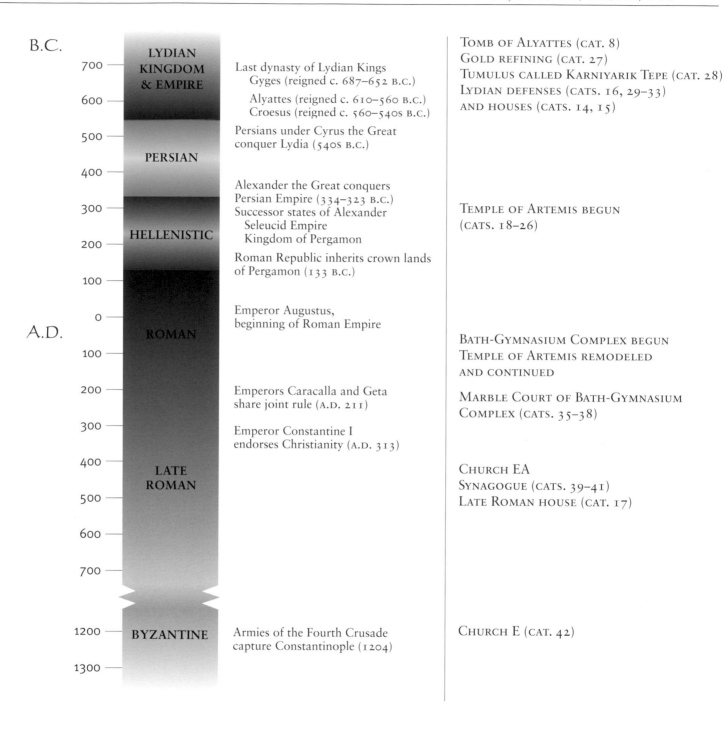

B.C.

700 — LYDIAN KINGDOM & EMPIRE

Last dynasty of Lydian Kings
   Gyges (reigned c. 687–652 B.C.)

600 —
   Alyattes (reigned c. 610–560 B.C.)
   Croesus (reigned c. 560–540s B.C.)

TOMB OF ALYATTES (CAT. 8)
GOLD REFINING (CAT. 27)
TUMULUS CALLED KARNIYARIK TEPE (CAT. 28)
LYDIAN DEFENSES (CATS. 16, 29–33)
AND HOUSES (CATS. 14, 15)

500 —

Persians under Cyrus the Great
conquer Lydia (540s B.C.)

PERSIAN

400 —

Alexander the Great conquers
Persian Empire (334–323 B.C.)

300 —
Successor states of Alexander
   Seleucid Empire
   Kingdom of Pergamon

TEMPLE OF ARTEMIS BEGUN
(CATS. 18–26)

HELLENISTIC

200 —

Roman Republic inherits crown lands
of Pergamon (133 B.C.)

100 —

0 —

Emperor Augustus,
beginning of Roman Empire

A.D.

ROMAN

100 —

BATH-GYMNASIUM COMPLEX BEGUN
TEMPLE OF ARTEMIS REMODELED
AND CONTINUED

200 —

Emperors Caracalla and Geta
share joint rule (A.D. 211)

MARBLE COURT OF BATH-GYMNASIUM
COMPLEX (CATS. 35–38)

300 —

Emperor Constantine I
endorses Christianity (A.D. 313)

400 —

LATE ROMAN

CHURCH EA
SYNAGOGUE (CATS. 39–41)
LATE ROMAN HOUSE (CAT. 17)

500 —

600 —

700 —

1200 — BYZANTINE

Armies of the Fourth Crusade
capture Constantinople (1204)

CHURCH E (CAT. 42)

1300 —

Introduction

Crawford H. Greenewalt, Jr., and Philip T. Stinson

Sardis, Sardeis, Sardes, Sparda, and Sart are all names of a settlement in Anatolia (western Asiatic Turkey; fig. 1) that had a long urban history and hosted many cultures. The settlement began more than three thousand years ago, in the middle of the second millennium B.C., if not before; for more than a millennium, from the seventh century B.C. until the seventh century A.D., Sardis was a major city of the ancient world. It survived through succeeding centuries, and still exists today. During its long existence, Sardis was host to many cultures: Mycenaean and Hittite, Lydian, Persian, Greek, Roman, Byzantine, Selcuk, and Ottoman, which followed one on another in a great pageant.

> *Think, in this batter'd Caravanserai*
> *Whose Doorways are alternate Night and Day,*
> *How Sultán after Sultán with his Pomp*
> *Abode his Hour or two, and went his way.*

Omar Khayyám, RUBÁIYÁT, Quatrain XVI, in Edward Fitzgerald's version

Sardis is located in one of the broad valleys of rivers that rise in the highlands of western Anatolia and empty into the Aegean Sea. Those valleys are separated by mountain ranges; and Sardis is located where river valley (the valley of the Hermus River; Turkish Gediz çayı) and mountain range (the range of Mt. Tmolus; Turkish Boz dağı) converge, in a landscape setting of dramatic contrasts (figs. 2, 3). A foothill that rises to an eminence of its own became the citadel, or Acropolis, of Sardis; flanking it are mountain streams, which flow into the plain and empty into the Hermus. One of those streams, west of the Acropolis, is the Pactolus (Turkish Sart çayı), which became famous in antiquity for its alluvial gold. The city grew up on the north side of the Acropolis, facing the river plain; cemeteries spread through the mountain stream valleys on either side. Another cemetery, much larger and dominated by the burial mounds (tumuli) of royalty and aristocracy, faced the city on a low ridge eleven kilometers (seven mi.) away, on the other side of the river valley; its Turkish name is Bin Tepe, meaning "thousand mounds." On the other side of Bin Tepe is a large lake, the Gygaean Lake (or Lake of Coloe; Turkish Marmara gölü).

Environment played a role in the emergence and continuity of settlement at Sardis. Some environmental features fulfilled basic requirements: the Acropolis was both a refuge and a stronghold; the Pactolus Stream a perennial source of fresh water; the Hermus Valley a vast fertile resource for

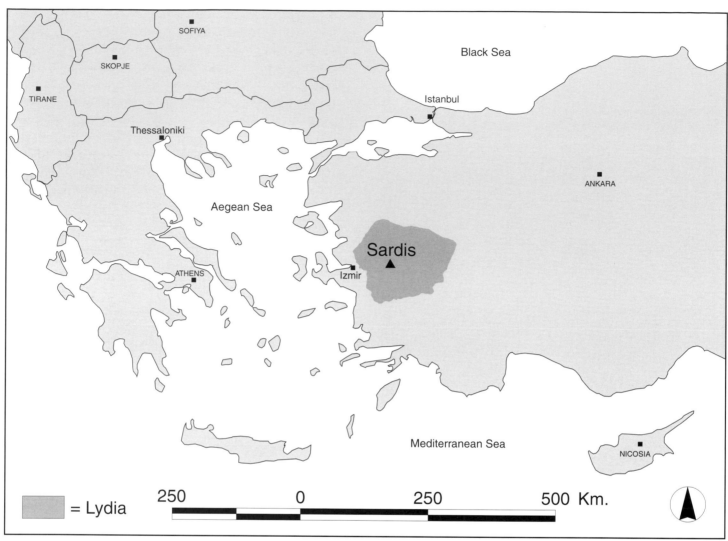

Fig. 1. Map of western Turkey, the Balkans, and Greece.

agriculture. Other features became assets after the settlement was established: the corridor of the river valley for communication between inland Anatolia and the Aegean; highland valleys on Mt. Tmolus for summer pasturage; alluvial gold in the Pactolus and other mountain streams on the north side of Tmolus for wealth, which became synonymous with Sardis.

The oldest occupation surfaces with related architecture that have been uncovered at Sardis are of the mid-second millennium B.C., when the settlement probably belonged to a region known as Seha River Land, alternately an independent kingdom and a dependency of the Hittite Empire. At that time, Sardis (or the Acropolis) may have been called

Hyde and people of the region Maeonians. In the *Iliad*, Maeonians are allies of Priam during the Trojan War, and "eddying Hermus," "snowy Tmolus," and the Gygaean Lake are their landmarks. Older artifacts, of the third millennium B.C. or Early Bronze Age, and of the Neolithic era, have been recovered out of context at the site; and Early Bronze Age cemeteries, and Neolithic and Paleolithic artifacts, have been recovered by the shores of the Gygaean Lake and at Bin Tepe. Beginning in the third millennium B.C. and continuing through antiquity and after, cultural material at Sardis shows affinities with both Greece and Anatolia. Ceramics of the second millennium B.C. include Mycenaean and Hittite forms; those of the early first

Those kings were famous for their wealth, especially in gold; two of them, Gyges and Croesus, also for mercurial fortunes. Croesus lost his throne and the Lydians their independence in the 540s B.C., when Lydia was conquered and Sardis captured by the Persians under their king Cyrus (Cyrus the Great). Thereafter, Sardis became the capital of a province of the Persian Empire, administered by viceroys, or satraps, who were often relatives of the Persian king. Persian rule ended with the conquests of Alexander the Great (who visited Sardis in 334 B.C.). During the Hellenistic era, which followed Alexander's death, the city was much coveted by his successors and their descendants, notably Seleucid dynasts, who ruled Syria and other parts of the Near East, and the kings of Pergamon. Under Roman rule, Sardis continued to be an important city, and in Late Roman times became capital of the Roman province of Lydia. The city declined in importance and size after the sixth century A.D., although its prestige lingered for another five hundred years: as late as the thirteenth century it was the site of a summit meeting between the Byzantine emperor and Turkish sultan. Between the eighteenth and twentieth centuries the settlement had dwindled to a small village, or group of villages; but since the founding of the Republic of Turkey it has revived and become a prosperous town, which still retains a form of the ancient name, Sart.

Research and excavation

Sardis has been explored and studied for forty-five years through a project called Archaeological Exploration of Sardis, or Sardis Expedition, which is cosponsored by the Harvard University Art Museums and Cornell University and which has its headquarters at Harvard University. Permission for fieldwork and research has been granted on an annual basis by the Turkish government, at present by the General Directorate of Monuments and Museums, which is a division of the Ministry of Culture. The Sardis Expedition was founded in 1958 by George M. A. Hanfmann (1911–1986), professor of fine arts at Harvard and John E. Hudson Professor of Archaeology. When the project began, Hanfmann was assisted by A. Henry Detweiler (1906–1970), professor of architecture and associate dean of the College of Architecture at Cornell University and at that time president of the American Schools of Oriental Research (which for many years was a Sardis Expedition sponsor). The primary aim of fieldwork at Sardis has been

Fig. 2. Sardis, view from the Acropolis, looking northwest (1973).

At the foot of the Acropolis is the reconstructed Marble Court of the Roman Bath-Gymnasium Complex, with the adjacent Late Roman Synagogue located on its south flank. Beyond is the valley of the Hermus River, and in the distance the cemetery of Bin Tepe, with its tumuli. The large tumulus at upper right is the tomb of King Alyattes of Lydia, father of Croesus.

millennium B.C., Greek and Anatolian Geometric decoration. By the seventh century B.C. if not before, Sardis had become the chief city of the Lydians, a native Anatolian people who spoke an Indo-European language, had distinctive cultural institutions of their own, and were very receptive to Greek culture. In the seventh and sixth centuries B.C., Lydian kings created an empire in western Anatolia—modest in size compared with other ancient empires, but rich in natural resources and at a historically and culturally important location between Greece and the Near East.

Fig. 3. Sardis, view to the Acropolis, looking south (1969).

In the foreground is part of the Late Roman Synagogue, partly reconstructed (its mosaic pavings not yet lifted and reset for display). On the other side of road is a low artificial hill, largely created by ruins of the Lydian city wall and extensively excavated after 1976. The macadam road in the foreground is the main highway connecting Ankara and Izmir. It is the successor to a sequence of roads, surfaces of which have been uncovered in excavations nearby: Ottoman, Byzantine, Roman, and Lydian, the last dating back at least to the seventh century B.C. The highway in the picture was replaced in 2001 by a new one, located north of the site, which ended a thoroughfare tradition at the older location of nearly three thousand years. (For excavation here in 1978, see frontispiece.)

to clarify the cultural history and urban development of the ancient city, as well as the culture of the Lydians, through mapping, excavation, and surveys of different kinds (surface sampling of artifacts, geomorphology, geophysics). Exploration and research at a site distinguished by long history, different cultures, and a wide range of archaeological conditions and artifact materials, sizes, and forms has also provided a training ground for topographers, excavators, historians, architects, conservators, and restorers.

The Harvard-Cornell project is the latest in a series of endeavors to explore and understand ancient Sardis.

Hanfmann's interest in Sardis stemmed partly from his research on the Etruscans (who, according to one ancient tradition, went to Italy from Lydia) and partly from a research legacy on Lydian pottery at Sardis, bequeathed by his senior colleague at Harvard, George H. Chase (1874–1952), professor of fine arts, dean of the Graduate School of Arts and Sciences, and ultimately dean of the University. Chase's legacy came from his membership in an earlier Sardis expedition, the Society for the Exploration of Sardis, active between 1910 and 1914 and in 1922, which had been founded and directed by Howard Crosby Butler

Fig. 4. Tumulus at Bin Tepe, locally called Koca Mutaf Tepe and identified as the Tomb of Alyattes, view looking north (1983). The Sardis Expedition Land Rover (presented to the Expedition by Landon Clay in 1964) provides a scale for the tumulus. The field in the foreground is planted in sesame.

(1872–1922), professor of the history of architecture at Princeton University. Excavation at Sardis by the Butler Expedition had focused on the Temple of Artemis (see the chapter "Crisp Lines") and on chamber tombs in the Pactolus Valley (the chamber tombs yielded much of the pottery that Chase and Hanfmann studied).

There had been earlier excavation in the Temple of Artemis: in 1904, by the Imperial Ottoman Museums in Constantinople, represented by Gustave Mendel (1873–1938); in 1882, by George Dennis (1814–1898; author of *Cities and Cemeteries of Etruria*);[1] and in 1750, by the team that included Robert Wood and Giovanni Battista Borra (see "Brush Strokes"). Little of the temple

architecture was uncovered in those efforts, however, owing to limited time and resources. At Bin Tepe, several burial mounds were excavated in the nineteenth century: in 1868–69 and 1882, by Dennis; and, earlier, in 1854, by Ludwig Peter Spiegelthal (1823–1900).[2] Spiegelthal excavated in the largest of the tumuli, plausibly identified as the tomb of Lydian king Alyattes, father of Croesus (figs. 2, 4; cat. 8); its burial chamber of huge, beautifully cut marble blocks (fig. 5) had been looted in antiquity (as were the chambers of all tumuli at Bin Tepe that have been excavated in modern times).

While the history of excavation at Sardis begins in the eighteenth century, with Robert Wood, research began much earlier, in the fifteenth century, with the visit of Cyriacus of Ancona in 1444. Roman tunneling in Lydian tumuli at Bin Tepe, to be sure, might conceivably have been stimulated in part by antiquarian concerns—since antiquarianism was popular in Roman times and for Romans Sardis held antiquarian interest, with its links to the alleged Lydian origin of the Etruscans and their major role in the early history of Rome.

Many ancient buildings at Sardis have always been partly visible above ground. One of those was the Temple of Artemis, and the impressive masonry construction and splendid ornament of its visible parts impressed visitors and stimulated their urge to draw or paint it. The Roman Bath-Gymnasium Complex also was partly visible, and it attracted attention because of its monumental size, high-quality materials, and handsome design features. Many buildings at Sardis, however, including ones of colossal size, became totally submerged below ground surface, their standing parts buried under fallen remains of their own superstructure, subsequent occupational materials, and natural deposits of alluvium and erosion; their only traces in the modern landscape were amorphous mounds and depressions, often barely distinguishable from natural features. One such building was the Synagogue (cats. 39–41; figs. 24, 28), the form, size, and identity of which came as a surprise after excavation began in 1962. Another example is the Lydian city wall (cats. 10, 29–33). Although several parts are twenty meters (sixty-five ft.) thick and still stand eight to ten meters high, and its circuit was more than three and a half kilometers (two mi.) long, and although its location is echoed by the Late Roman city wall (stretches of which rise above modern ground surface), Lydian city wall remains were entirely unsuspected for the first eighteen excavation seasons of the Harvard-Cornell Expedition. Its discovery and identification illustrate the fortuitous circumstances and interpretive problems of much archaeological fieldwork.

The Lydian city wall was discovered during the field season of 1976, by longtime Expedition members Nancy and Andrew Ramage, in the course of a late afternoon stroll. Prior to their discovery, the low hill across the road from the Synagogue had attracted little attention by Expedition members, many of whom uncritically dismissed it as a natural feature. In 1976, the Expedition was looking for a source of clay (with which to make facsimiles of Lydian roof and decorative tiles, for a touristic display). Andrew Ramage knew that villagers of Sart had often quarried in the hill scarp (created c. 1950, when highway widening removed the north side of the hill) to obtain clayey material for making mudbrick, or adobe, which they used for house construction. Thinking that the hill might provide clay appropriate for Expedition needs, Ramage stopped to investigate the scarp. From his long excavation experience, he quickly recognized the faint but regular horizontal and vertical divisions that represented joints in masonry construction, realized that the clayey material was not a natural formation but a monumental mudbrick structure, and guessed that the building belonged to the city wall of Lydian times. Subsequent excavation confirmed his (very educated!) guess (see frontispiece).

In this location, the city wall was reinforced on its west side by a massive earthwork (well preserved in the west side of the hill). For many years after 1976, the orientation of the wall was uncertain: did it protect city to the west and face east, or protect city to the east and face west? A passage in the *History* of Herodotus (5.101), which suggests that the Pactolus Stream—located west of the wall—flowed through the city, supports the former orientation, the many substantial Roman building remains east of the Lydian wall support the latter. The earthwork might have been either an external glacis or an internal *agger*. Lydian architecture and occupation remains existed on both sides of the wall, attesting extramural as well as intramural occupation, and on either side could be either extramural or intramural. The discovery and excavation, in 1999 and 2000, of Lydian city wall segments elsewhere in the city site (to the south and east) showed that this segment protected city core to the east and faced west (strengthened by an earthwork glacis) and that in most places the location of the Lydian circuit was identical to that of the Late Roman city wall, built a thousand years later.

Ancient buildings and excavation sectors are referred to by letter designations, which were introduced by the Butler and Harvard-Cornell Expeditions. Single letters of the alphabet, A through H, which the Butler Expedition gave to unexcavated monuments (cat. 43), were meant to be clearly noncommittal with respect to function and era. On excavation, Building B proved to be a Roman bath-gymnasium complex (to which the Marble Court belongs); Building E is a Byzantine church. The acronyms and abbreviations that the Harvard-Cornell Expedition uses for excavation sectors,

Fig. 5. Tumulus at Bin Tepe called Koca Mutaf Tepe, the Tomb of Alyattes (1993).

The view, taken inside the tumulus, shows the doorway to the tomb chamber from the outside, where a forecourt is framed by a pair of huge limestone blocks; one of the blocks is partly visible at left. The walls of the chamber are marble, the ceiling blocks limestone. The front ceiling block (visible here) is nearly 3.90 meters (12 ft. 9 in.) long, 1.11 meters (3 ft. 8 in.) high, and 1.45 meters (4 ft. 9 in.) thick on its underside. The scale figure is Christopher Ratté.

however, stand for names that often embody Expedition assumptions about function and era: Sector MMS, for Monumental Mudbrick Structure, was introduced before the dominant structure of that sector was generally agreed to be a defense work and before its stone construction had been exposed (and sectors MMS/N and MMS/S are located respectively to its north and south); Sector ByzFort, for

Byzantine Fort or Fortress, was named for a dominant structure that proved to be neither Byzantine nor a fort/fortress; and Sector PN stands for Pactolus North. Columns of the Temple of Artemis were given numbers by the Butler Expedition, and surviving column capitals were given letters (see fig. 17). Artemis Temple columns are designated by the Butler Expedition numbers in this catalogue.

Topography and monuments clarified by site exploration and excavation supplement the ancient historical and literary records of Sardis with the vivid and explicit testimony of space and form. This exhibition presents some of that testimony: the huge funeral mound of Croesus's father, King Alyattes, 355 meters (1165 ft.) in diameter (cat. 8; figs. 4, 5); from Croesus's reign, the massive Lydian city wall (20 m thick) and adjacent houses, with dramatic evidence for their sack by the Persians (cats. 14, 16, 29–33), and Lydian installations for refining silver and gold (cat. 27); the Hellenistic-Roman Temple of Artemis, one of the largest Greek-style temples, with superbly designed and executed Ionic ornament (cats. 19–21, 23; figs. 6–11, 13, 19); a grand imperial Roman Bath-Gymnasium Complex that combines Greek and Roman traditions of function and design (cats. 35–38; figs. 24–27); and three or four churches and the largest synagogue of antiquity (cats. 22, 39–42; figs. 24, 28, 29).

Aim of the exhibition

This exhibition concerns the topographical landscape and historical architecture of Sardis and their graphic recording since the middle of the eighteenth century. The architecture belongs to the Lydian, Hellenistic, Roman, and Byzantine eras; earlier and later eras (before the first millennium B.C., and the fourteenth century A.D. and later) are not represented because their occupation remains uncovered to date lack complex and monumental architecture. (Graphic records of small-scale artifacts such as painted pottery also were considered for the exhibition, but were rejected mainly because of space limitations.) The exhibition features original drawings insofar as possible. Some originals, however, were unavailable for loan (like those in the sketchbook by Giovanni Battista Borra, figs. 6–9, 12–14); others would have occupied too much exhibition space (like cat. 24, the Temple of Artemis plan at a scale of 1:20, which in totality would be nearly five meters [sixteen ft.] long—and would require elimination of drawing sheet margins) and are reproduced at reduced scale.

Architectural and topographical features of the site have attracted visitors for different reasons and have been approached in different ways and with different objectives, partly stimulated by changes in attitudes toward antiquity and by developments in technology. By "graphic recording" we mean the conventional language of drawing that explains significant features of the archaeology, monuments, and landscapes of Sardis. Graphic conventions are only successful when they effectively communicate the intent of the recorder. The drawings in this exhibition were selected because they succeed in communicating their creators' intent. The instruments and methods of graphic communication also affect aims and goals. Computer-aided graphic representational tools, such as computer-aided design (CAD), are becoming more flexible and productive than previous methods, and new digital techniques are expanding traditional aims of graphic recording at Sardis.

In the eighteenth and nineteenth centuries, graphic recording of Greek and Roman monuments typically aimed to provide models that would improve the design and ornament of contemporaneous architecture, or to relate landscape and architecture with historical events, or to evoke through images of ruin and destruction the romance of the past and the sadness of irrevocable loss. The chapter title "Brush Strokes" refers to the graphic conventions of early visitors, who created renderings with colored ink washes over lines of pencil and ink on paper. "Brush Strokes" also functions as a metaphor for the romantic spirit of antiquarianism, which stimulated the visitation and exploration of ancient sites of the Mediterranean and Near East by westerners. In the nineteenth and twentieth centuries, recording became more catholic and documented ancient monuments regardless of their perceived artistic merit, historical significance, or dramatic qualities. Many drawings are extremely precise, showing assemblage details, technical features, and damaged parts that have potential value for understanding

history and use (as in stone-by-stone "state" plans, elevations, and sections; e.g., cats. 16, 24). "Crisp Lines" refers to the tradition of drawing with hard, fine lines that developed in the nineteenth century, when archaeological methods became more systematic and scientific. "Crisp Lines" symbolizes the ideal expression of accuracy, clarity, and consistency in drawing conventions, with no preference for aesthetic achievement or subjects from a particular cultural period. Some drawings are analytical (cat. 2), highly interpretive, and aim to clarify through simplification, or to test ideas through experimental reconstruction. "Dashed Lines," our third rubric, signifies reconstruction or restoration, a dashed line being the simplest graphic convention for indicating the trace, position, or spatial configuration of something that no longer exists. Reconstruction drawings and computer models attempt to recreate the condition of a structure before alteration or destruction. Much architectural and topographical evidence has become accessible only in the late twentieth century, with the computer, electronic transits, and Global Positioning System (GPS) equipment. "Infinite Points," the title of the final chapter, is a metaphor for the new electronic and computerized technologies that are dramatically changing the graphic recording of Sardis, and opening a new window on its complex urban history. Computer reconstructions permit and encourage comprehensive study, as do full-scale physical reconstructions (figs. 24, 27, 28); unlike the latter, however, they allow easy exploration of alternatives, do not compromise original evidence, and are less expensive. Computer reconstructions by themselves, however, lack the human palpability that invites response in hand-drawn graphics.

The two images of the Theater and Stadium at Sardis in catalogue numbers 1A and 2 illustrate approaches in graphic recording of the mid-eighteenth and early twenty-first centuries. The first, of about 1750 (cat. 1A), is a perspective view, naturalistic and probably accurate (because the artist was an architect and engineer, and belonged to a research team committed to accurate recording); it is valuable for its artistic quality and for its explicit record of contemporaneous features and conditions. Perspective drawings done solely for the purpose of recording archaeological remains are not common today; they are reserved for restoring or reconstructing ancient monuments (see "Dashed Lines"). The artist, Giovanni Battista Borra, however, successfully communicated the basic configuration of the Theater and Stadium in one *veduta*. The watercolor also illustrates how important landscapes and geographical settings were to Borra and his contemporaries.

The drawing from 2003 in cat. 2 is a plan made with the aid of computer technologies and incorporating the results of geophysical survey; it is valuable for information about the topographical setting of the Theater and its design relationship to the adjacent Stadium, and for evidence (provided by topographical contours as well as by geophysical survey) of artificial terracing and other features below present-day ground surface near the Stadium. When juxtaposed with Borra's small but colorful and lively drawing, the computer-generated plan may seem cold and impalpable. Although the border, grid lines, and other graphic conventions manifest vestiges of the traditional methodology of drawing at the drafting board, human hands did not physically create a single element of the image. Advantages of this approach to graphic recording lie in its inherent precision and in the capabilities of its computer database, which can also generate different kinds of representations of the same features, such as elevations, sections, three-dimensional orthographic projections, and perspectives. Graphic representations of Sardis topography today tend to be more analytical by modern standards than those of Borra and other early recorders of the site, but they can also be visually compelling.

1. On the 1904 excavation, see Mendel 1905; on 1882, see Rhodes 1973, 146–47.
2. On Dennis, see Rhodes 1973, 100–107, 146; on Spiegelthal, see Olfers 1854 and Olfers 1859.

1A

VIEW OF THE THEATER AT SARDIS

Giovanni Battista Borra (Italian, 1713–1770), c. 1750

Watercolor with pen and black ink over graphite
on laid paper

15.9 × 20.3 cm (6¼ × 8 in.), image

Yale Center for British Art, Paul Mellon Collection,
B1977.14.929A

Published in Vann 1989, fig. 89.

1B

PLAN OF THE EAST END OF THE TEMPLE OF ARTEMIS AT SARDIS

Giovanni Battista Borra, c. 1750

Pen and black ink over graphite on laid paper

15.9 × 20.3 cm (6¼ × 8 in.), image

Yale Center for British Art, Paul Mellon Collection,
B1977.14.929B

A (above): The Theater, together with the Stadium of Sardis, is located on lower north slopes of the Acropolis on the east side of the city. The two buildings form an integrated unit, oriented at right angles to each other (see also cat. 3). Neither has been excavated; and many parts of both buildings, including their seats and remains of the Theater's stage facade (*scaenae frons*) probably survive under a thick deposit of earth that has accumulated over time and has eroded from the Acropolis above. The Theater had an estimated seating capacity of about 12,000 to 15,000 (compare theaters at Ephesus, 25,000; Miletos, 15,000; Pergamon, 10,000; Athens, Theater of Dionysos, 17,000; Epidauros, 13,000–14,000).

This is a view looking south, showing the auditorium *cavea* and retaining *parodos* walls (labeled A and B). The Theater looks much the same today as it did two and a half centuries ago, when this watercolor was made. The arched opening (C) in the center of the *cavea* survives today in the form of an amorphous lump of mortared brick and rubble. The arches of the Stadium's curved end (*sphendone*) are in the view on the left side (E).

B: The temple was identified as a temple of Artemis only after excavation by the Butler Expedition in 1910 had recovered inscriptional evidence on the building and on adjacent dedications. Borra's plan shows walls and columns of the east end of the temple. Those visible above ground are crosshatched (including columns with Butler numbers 1, 6, 7, 10, 16, and 17 [see fig. 17], the northeast anta, and parts of the long north and south walls and cross wall); those conjectured are simple-hatched. Borra and his companions correctly understood that the Temple was octastyle (with eight columns on the short ends). They excavated at the column labeled E to expose its base, and lines in the drawing indicate excavation on the west side of that column (number 16; see fig. 9). Absent in the plan are the two central columns of the inner porch (numbers 11 and 12; they are the ones that have unusual pedestals, which have been the subject of much discussion). Those columns appear in Borra's notebook sketch, but in outline and with single lines through each, as if they were at first hypothesized and later rejected by the artist. (Borra's notebook sketch also shows two nonexistent columns of an inner south colonnade, one of them crosshatched with a cross through it, the other in outline.) The scale is in feet. Borra's views of the Temple ruins appear in cat. 4 and fig. 13.   CHG

2

Theater and Stadium of Sardis and their environs, plan of visible remains

Philip T. Stinson, James M. Toris, 2003

Computer-generated drawing

Archaeological Exploration of Sardis, M-136

Measurements taken with a total station electronic transit reveal a precise design relationship between the two buildings: if the semicircular end (*sphendone*) of the Stadium were extended to form a complete circle, the point on the circle opposite the midpoint of the *sphendone* would be tangent to the axis of the Theater *cavea*. This relationship was not apparent from the visible ruins.

Although a second hemicycle *sphendone* is shown also at the west end of the Stadium in two drawings of the late nineteenth and early twentieth centuries, no other evidence for a west-end hemicycle is known.

The plan also shows a temple of the first century A.D. (Wadi B Temple on the current master plan; see cat. 44), a spur of the Acropolis terraced in the sixth century B.C. and occupied in the sixth century B.C. and in Roman times (Sector ByzFort), and, in the west end of the Stadium and beyond, preliminary results of a geophysical magnetic survey over an area of 1.7 hectares (4.2 acres). The survey was conducted by geophysicists from Ninth of September University in Izmir in 2001, and also used resistivity and seismic techniques; it aimed to clarify subsurface architecture and other features through noninvasive exploratory techniques, and revealed terrace walls and other features that remain to be identified.   CHG

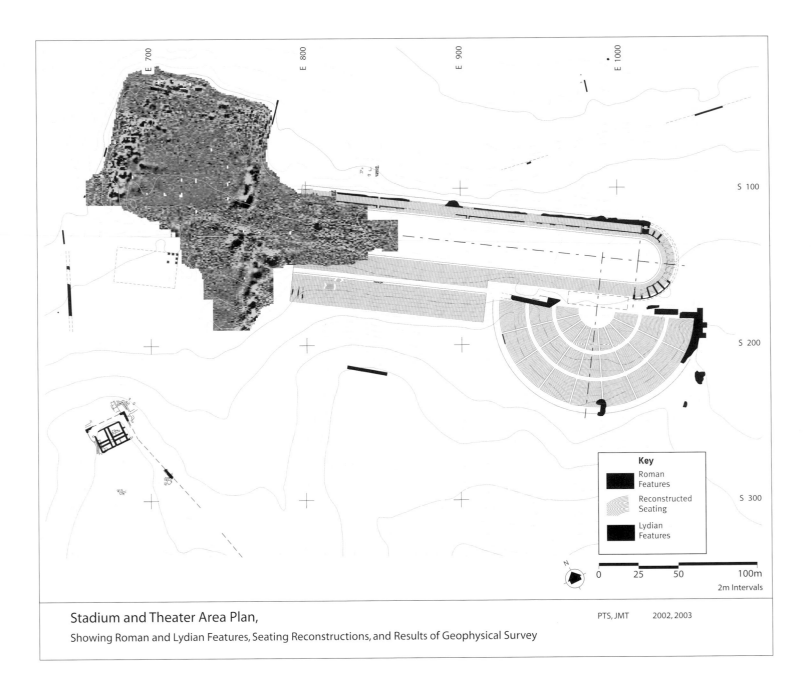

E 700 **E 800** **E 900** **E 1000**

S 100

S 200

S 300

Key

Roman Features

Reconstructed Seating

Lydian Features

N

0 25 50 100m

2m Intervals

Stadium and Theater Area Plan,
Showing Roman and Lydian Features, Seating Reconstructions, and Results of Geophysical Survey

PTS, JMT   2002, 2003

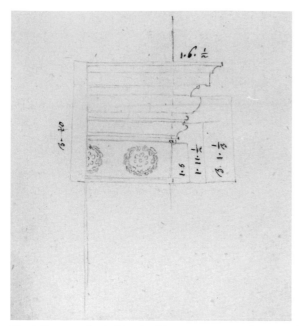

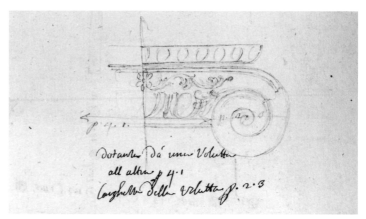

Fig. 8. Borra notebook, Temple of Artemis, one-half volute side of capital on column number 6.

Giovanni Battista Borra, notebook p. 51, graphite and ink on wove paper. Joint Library of the Hellenic and Roman Societies, London.

This shows the same column as in fig. 7.

Fig. 6. Borra notebook, Temple of Artemis, anta capital, measured drawing.

Giovanni Battista Borra (Italian, 1713–1770), 27 May–2 June 1750, notebook p. 54, graphite and ink on wove paper, 31.4 × 20.4 cm (12⅜ × 8 in.; dimensions of all notebook pages reproduced). Joint Library of the Hellenic and Roman Societies, London.

John Bouverie's notebook records that "ye Capital of ye Pilaster is beautiful & unusual ye joints of all ye stones remarkably well polish'd & set together & ye wall extending from ye Pilaster buniato" (Hutton 1927, 107).

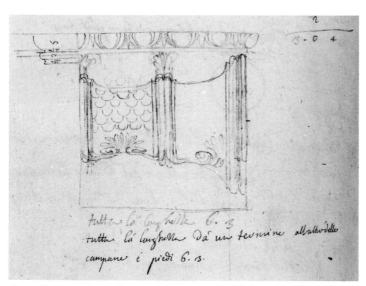

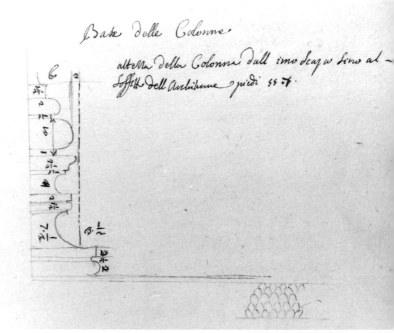

Fig. 9. Borra notebook, Temple of Artemis, profile of base of column number 16, exposed in excavation by Wood.

Giovanni Battista Borra, notebook p. 56, graphite and ink on wove paper. Joint Library of the Hellenic and Roman Societies, London.

The official diary of Wood's party records that "the exquisite Tast of the Capitals & most excellent Workmanship invited Us to resolve (by digging) to get at the Members &ca" (Hutton 1927, 105). The column by which excavation took place is labeled E in the plan in cat. 1B, and A in the elevation in cat. 4. "We dug down about ft. 22 [23 ft. 5 in.] to discover ye Base of a Pillar wh found a good deal different from ye regular Ionic Base, consisting of more Members & less Projection most likely to disencumber ye spaces as much as possible" (Bouverie's notebook; Hutton 1927, 107; with commentary, 108–9).

Fig. 7. Borra notebook, Temple of Artemis, one-half bolster side of capital on column number 6.

Giovanni Battista Borra, notebook p. 51, graphite and ink on wove paper. Joint Library of the Hellenic and Roman Societies, London.

In the descriptive account by Bouverie, the capital is identified with the one now numbered 6 (Hutton 1927, 107).

Brush Strokes

Crawford H. Greenewalt, Jr.

Graphic recording of historical landscapes and monuments at Sardis begins with travelers from western Europe, who visited the site from the fifteenth through the nineteenth century; some of them also conducted limited excavation. "Brush Strokes" stands for those images (which in fact were presented in a variety of techniques, including pencil and pen and ink, as well as watercolor). Early travelers' interest in Sardis reflects the high status enjoyed by classical antiquity in the West, and the belief that a better understanding of Greece and Rome would benefit western European culture. Sardis was one of many ancient sites of the Mediterranean world recorded by travelers. Like many others, it was relatively accessible—approximately one hundred kilometers (about sixty mi.) inland from the commercial port city of Smyrna (modern Izmir)—and it had played a central role in Greek and Roman history; in addition, it had been the chief city of a native Anatolian people, the Lydians, whose kings had created a mighty empire in what is today western Turkey, and whose names were bywords for fabulous wealth.

The drawings were prepared and finished for different purposes. The earliest travelers' main concern was to record for posterity what they saw, particularly architecture and inscriptions on stone. Many travelers of the eighteenth and early nineteenth centuries also had a pedagogical interest, to improve architectural taste in their own countries through exposure to the models of Greece and Rome; their drawings regularly include carefully measured plans, sections, and details (e.g., figs. 6–9). Celebrated architects and architectural historians who visited Sardis and made drawings of its monuments include Charles Robert Cockerell (1788–1863; cat. 5) and Auguste Choisy (1841–1909). Sardis seems not to have been chosen for illustration by prizewinning architects (envois) from the École des Beaux-Arts in Paris, who created the splendid large-scale panoramic renderings of monuments in their settings at other sites. In the 1920s, however, after the Temple of Artemis had been excavated by the Butler Expedition, the Beaux-Arts style was used by Edwin Avery Park (1891–1978) and Maitland Belknap (1889–1958), respectively, for the restored plan of the Temple and for design features of an interior column (columns 11, 12; figs. 10, 17). Some nineteenth-century drawings were made for picture books aimed at readers primarily interested in historical or religious aspects of the site—for example, Sardis as one of the Seven Churches of Asia (Book of Revelation 1.11)—and readily satisfied by romantic

Vol II Plate C

ONE METER.

DETAILS OF CAPITALS Nos 11 AND 12.

Fig. 10. Details of columns 11 and 12, published by the Butler Expedition (Butler 1925, Text, pl. C).

Maitland Belknap, before 1923.

views and landscapes (cats. 6, 7; fig. 11). In them verticality may be exaggerated, viewpoints conflated, and monuments juxtaposed for dramatic effect.

The first antiquarian traveler to Sardis we know of was Cyriacus of Ancona (1391–1452?), who came in April 1444 (nine years before Constantinople fell to the Ottoman Turks). He panned for gold in the Pactolus Stream, recorded several inscriptions on stone, and described the Temple of Artemis: "I observed a portion of an extraordinarily elegant wall belonging to the impressive temple of Sardian Jove, and surviving to our own day, twelve round, huge columns 45 feet tall and 15 feet in circumference,

standing in their [original] positions."[1] Cyriacus's discovery at Sardis of an inscription honoring a priest of Zeus Polieus[2] may have prompted his association of the Temple with Jove. If Cyriacus made drawings at Sardis, as he did at other sites, they no longer survive.

The earliest surviving drawings of Sardis include those made in 1750 by Giovanni Battista Borra (1713–1770), the artist of an expedition whose other members were the Irishman Robert Wood (1716–1771) and the Englishmen James Dawkins (1722–1757) and John Bouverie (c. 1722–1750). A notebook with nineteen pages of Borra's pencil drawings illustrating Sardis monuments is now in London (Institute of Classical Studies, Joint Library of the Hellenic and Roman Societies; figs. 6–9, 12–14); eight sheets of his finished drawings are in New Haven (Yale Center for British Art; cats. 1, 3, 4; fig. 15). Wood, Borra, and their companions traveled in Anatolia and Syria to record topography and ancient architecture;[3] their records of Palmyra and Baalbek were published, and the publications had a significant impact on design in neoclassical architecture.[4] Had Borra's drawings of Sardis been finished and published, the beautiful Ionic column capitals and bases of the Temple of Artemis, which were greatly admired by expedition members, might also have become part of the neoclassical design repertory. The first scholarly excavation at Sardis on record was made by the team of Wood and Borra. They excavated by the column immediately east of the northeast anta (end of the porch wall), evidently on its west side, to expose the column base (the column is labeled E in cat. 1B, A in cat. 4, and 16 in fig. 17; Borra's sketch of the base is shown in fig. 9).

Charles Robert Cockerell (1788–1863), who visited Sardis in 1812, is remembered today for his recording and excavation of the Temples of Aphaia on Aegina and of Apollo at Bassae, his rediscovery of entasis (the convex curvature in the profile of Greek column shafts), and for some of his architecture (e.g., the Ashmolean Museum, Oxford). Auguste Choisy (1841–1909) visited Sardis and Bin Tepe in 1875; at Sardis he recorded two large Roman buildings, which he identified—perhaps rightly—as churches,[5] and at Bin Tepe he recorded tumulus chamber tombs and their couches.[6] Choisy is remembered today for his magisterial history of architecture, published in 1899.[7]

Early travelers' drawings are valuable for their record of loss and survival. In the Temple of Artemis, six columns and an anta stood complete or near complete and two

Fig. 11. Ruins of the Temple of Artemis.

Clarkson Frederick Stanfield, R.A. (British, 1793–1867), c. 1835, graphite, watercolor, and gouache, heightened with white, 23.3 × 35.5 cm (9⅛ × 14 in.). Victoria and Albert Museum, Searight Drawing 1000.

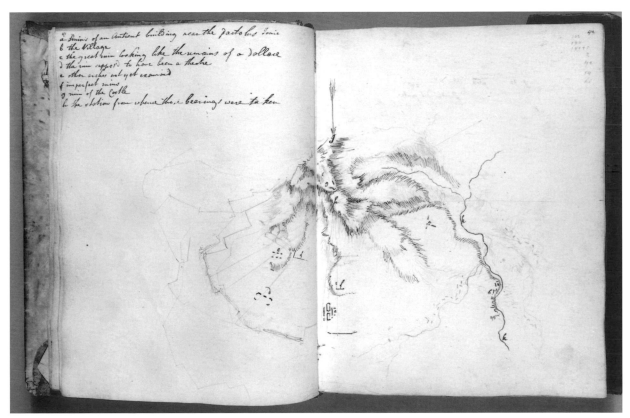

Fig. 12. Borra notebook, map of Sardis.

Giovanni Battista Borra, 27 May–2 June 1750, notebook pp. 41–42, graphite and ink on wove paper. Joint Library of the Hellenic and Roman Societies, London.

Fig. 13. Borra notebook, Temple of Artemis, view looking south.

Giovanni Battista Borra, notebook p. 58, graphite and ink on wove paper. Joint Library of the Hellenic and Roman Societies, London.

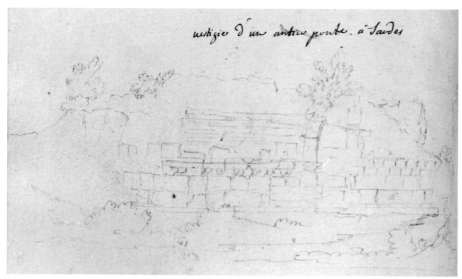

Fig. 14. Borra notebook, Bridge over Pactolus Stream, view looking east.

Giovanni Battista Borra, notebook, p. 43, graphite and ink on wove paper. Joint Library of the Hellenic and Roman Societies, London.

Labeled "vestigie d'un antico ponte a Sardes." Ruins of the bridge still exist, but without the stone facing shown in Borra's drawings (see also fig. 15). In the mid-1950s, the ruins supported wooden beams that carried traffic across the stream (see Hanfmann 1983, 47–49).

Fig. 15. "View of a Ruined Bridge."

Giovanni Battista Borra, c. 1750, watercolor with pen and black and gray ink on laid paper 15.9 × 20.3 cm (6¼ × 8 in.), image. Yale Center for British Art, Paul Mellon Collection, B1977.14.958B.

architrave blocks were in their original position when Borra made his 1750 sketch and subsequent drawing (cat. 4; fig. 13; compare twelve columns seen by Cyriacus, cited above); only five of those stood by the end of 1750; three columns were complete when Cockerell visited in 1812 (cat. 5); and only two—those that still stand—in 1824, when Anton von Prokesch (1795–1876) visited Sardis.[8] The bridge over the Pactolus Stream has lost the vaulting and consoles that it had when Borra drew it (figs. 14, 15). The Theater, on the other hand, looks much the same today as it does in Borra's drawing (cat. 1A).

1. Cyriac of Ancona forthcoming.
2. Buckler and Robinson 1932, 63–64, no. 47.
3. Wood 1753, page a recto; Wiebenson 1969, 30–33; Constantine 1984, 66–84.
4. Crook 1972, 72–73.
5. Choisy 1883, 160–61.
6. Choisy 1876.
7. Choisy 1899.
8. Prokesch von Osten 1837, 32.

3

"PLAN OF THE CITY OF SARDIS WITH
SEVERAL VESTIGES OF MANY ANCIENT
BUILDINGS, STILL EXTANT IN THE YEAR
1750"

Giovanni Battista Borra (Italian, 1713–1770), c. 1750

Pen and gray and black ink with gray wash over
graphite on laid paper

20.3 × 31.8 cm (8 × 12½ in.), image

Yale Center for British Art, Paul Mellon Collection,
B1977.14.928

Published in Vann 1989, fig. 6.

The earliest known map of Sardis was
drawn by Borra in 1750. Arriving at the
site from the main road along the edge of
the Hermus Plain, the visitor naturally
looks up to the south toward the Tmolus
Mountains; south seems naturally "up" at
Sardis. Probably for this reason, both
Borra and the Butler Expedition (cat. 43)
chose to orient their maps with south at
the top of the map, the reverse of the usual
orientation.

Borra's map is depicted as a curled,
torn, and wrinkled field sheet—a state familiar to most users of maps; its right side
is pinned to a board, while the left twists
free. The rugged topography of the site is
indicated with delicate brush strokes, giving a clear impression of the rocky cliffs
that separate the Acropolis from the lower
city, the terraces of the lower town, and
the chain of mounds along the north side
of the city (between the Roman buildings
labeled here H and K, and the eighteenth-
century road M). Both modern and ancient buildings are indicated—including
the yet-unexcavated standing columns of
the Temple of Artemis (D), the Theater (F)
and Stadium (G, showing the underground
vaulting of the Stadium, which Borra must
have explored), the Bath-Gymnasium
Complex (H), the Byzantine remains on
the Acropolis, and other buildings.

Borra's map of the urban area of Sardis
was probably based on a known preliminary drawing (fig. 12). However, comparison of the final and preliminary versions
raises some interesting questions. We can
be confident that Borra prepared the

preliminary drawing on the site, because
of the light lines that radiate out from a
central location on the Acropolis. These
lines suggest the drawing was created
using some kind of surveying instrument,
perhaps an early form of the alidade (see
cat. 9A). Laying a digital scan of the final
map over a scan of the preliminary drawing, however, reveals several discrepancies.
For instance, the locations and orienta-
tions of major monuments, such as the
Temple of Artemis, Stadium, Theater, the
buildings today called Buildings C and D
(see cat. 43), and the Roman Bath-Gymnasium Complex are slightly different on
each map. Additionally, some significant
features shown on the final version, such
as the east-west road, do not appear on
the preliminary version. Some features,
confusingly, are depicted more astutely on
the preliminary map. For instance, the relationship of the orientation of the Theater
and Stadium (F and G on the final; not labeled on the preliminary) to the other
standing monuments in the lower city area
to the north (down) is depicted more accurately on the preliminary version. Other
evidence suggests that the limiting lines of
the final version were not established by
simply tracing over or copying those of the
preliminary sketch. Several features on the
final version were obviously erased and
shifted, including the Stadium (G) and two
preserved segments of the Roman city wall
(E) east of the Stadium. These observa-
tions suggest that the final version required
at least one more drawing with additional
information (now lost?). Obvious discrepancies are more difficult to explain. One
might have assumed that Borra would
have closely followed the preliminary field
drawing in the final version. His memory
and general feelings of the site, however,
may have influenced his final rendering of
the Sardis landscape and even the placement of its major landmarks. Fortunately,
we have good documentation of another
instance where Borra changed his preliminary sketch for the final version, in his
veduta of the Temple of Artemis (see next
entry). NDC, PTS

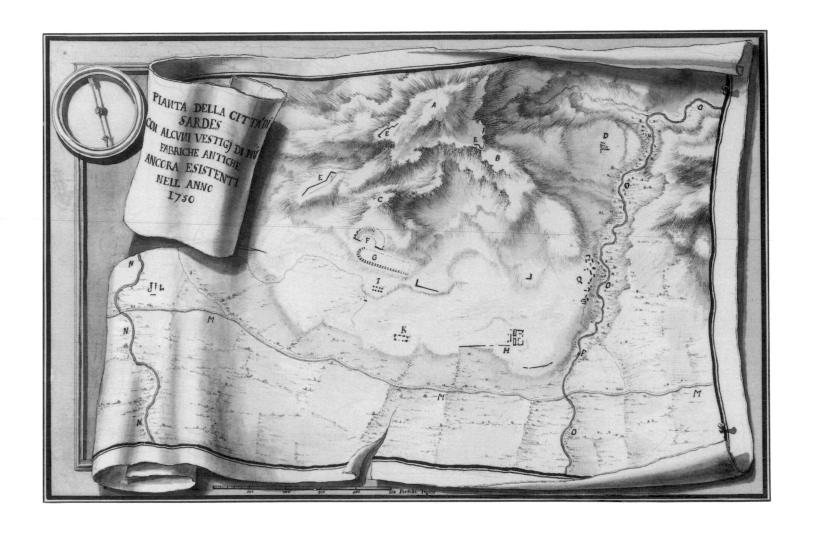

PIANTA DELLA CITTA DI
SARDES
CON ALCVNI VESTIGJ DI PIV
FABRICHE ANTICHE
ANCORA ESISTENTI
NELL ANNO
1750

"VIEW OF THE RUINS OF AN IONIC TEMPLE AT SARDIS"

Giovanni Battista Borra, c. 1750

Gray wash with pen and gray and black ink over graphite on laid paper

20.7 × 31.8 cm (8⅛ × 12½ in.), image

Yale Center for British Art, Paul Mellon Collection, B1977.14.959

Published in Scott 2001, fig. 3.

This ink-wash drawing by Giovanni Battista Borra based on a pencil sketch probably made at the site shows the east porch of the Temple of Artemis viewed from the northeast, as it appeared at the end of May of 1750. The pencil sketch is in a notebook now in the Joint Library of the Hellenic and Roman Societies in London (fig. 13). Borra was the draftsman for Robert Wood's small party of four on their famous travels to Palmyra and Baalbek in 1750–51 (the other two members were John Bouverie and James Dawkins, both recent Oxford graduates). It appears that Borra recorded the same intact six columns seen by Thomas Smith when he visited Sardis in 1670 (Smith did not specify the columns or produce a drawing).[1] Perhaps the first western traveler to set his eyes on the famed and beautiful temple when it was substantially more complete was Cyriacus of Ancona, who visited Sardis in April 1444, some three centuries before Wood, and marveled at the "impressive temple of Sardian Jove," and its surviving "twelve round, huge columns . . . in their [original] positions."[2] The columns shown in this drawing are numbers 1, 6, and 7, on the east front (the first three columns from the left); numbers 10 and 16, carrying two lengths of the architrave spanning between them and the northeast anta pier; and number 17, the column directly in front of the southeast anta, shown in the distance, between the latter two (the numbering system devised by Bouverie and developed by Butler continues to be used by the current excavation; see fig. 17).

All of the columns, except number 1, retain their capitals (the capital for number 1 is shown at the foot of the column, upended), and the capital of number 6 is askew, as it still is. Today, only two columns, numbers 6 and 7, are preserved fully, and look much like the way they do in the Borra drawing. The columns are shown uniformly preserved nine to ten courses (drums) above the ground level, or about one-half of their total height. When Howard Crosby Butler started the excavation of the Temple in 1910, the ground was some one to one and a half meters lower, perhaps the result of erosion, but more likely from illicit digging for the Temple's coveted marble elements. A sketch plan made on the site, where the surviving columns are shown as cross-hatched circles (cat. 1B is a finished version of this sketch), and the written account in Bouverie's diary corroborate the drawing and indicate that Wood's party had worked out the basic architectural arrangement of the east porch correctly. It appears that the remains of the Temple impressed and fascinated the group and there was much desire to learn more about it. During the six days they stayed at Sardis (27 May–2 June) they, or hired locals, dug down all the way to the base of column 16 (left or east of the northeast anta in the drawing, where it is labeled A)—the first historically recorded excavations at the Temple—and sketched what appeared to them the unusual Ionic-Attic profile of the base and the vertical leaf decoration of its torus (fig. 9): "ye upper Toro was adorn'd with scales pointed upwards."[3]

Although Borra's drawing is remarkably accurate, he has taken some liberties, varying his vantage point in order to create a "maximum view" and reveal more of the features of the Temple. One such minor inconsistency, visible because Borra shifted his vantage point eastward, is of invaluable help to us: the architrave carried by column number 10 (labeled B) reveals its east face with a profile molding of two fasciae and a simple crown molding, albeit at a very narrow perspective. This detail confirms that the projecting inner porch ends with column number 10—its northeast corner column—and that therefore, the outside corners of the porch were carried by regular Ionic capitals facing east-west like the rest of the capitals of the porch, not special corner Ionic capitals, as one would have expected.

Claude Charles de Peyssonnel, who visited Sardis only a few months after Wood and recorded the same general view, shows only five intact columns.[4] Apparently, in the brief time between the two visits, column number 17, in front of the southeast anta (between the columns labeled A and B), had been razed to the ground.   FKY

1. Smith 1674, 136–37; Smith 1676, 27–32.
2. Cyriac of Ancona forthcoming.
3. Hutton 1927, 107, pl. XIX.
4. Peyssonnel 1765, 336–37.

5

SKETCH OF THE ARTEMIS TEMPLE AT
SARDIS (GLUED INTO COCKERELL'S
COPY OF "ANTIQUITIES OF IONIA" BY
RICHARD CHANDLER, NICHOLAS
REVETT, AND WILLIAM PARS [1769],
OPPOSITE PLATE IV, THE TEMPLE OF
ATHENA AT PRIENE)

Charles Robert Cockerell (British, 1788–1863), 1812

Graphite on cream wove paper

27 × 41.5 cm (10¾ × 16⅜ in.)

Yale Center for British Art, Paul Mellon Collection,
Folio A/N/128/copy 2

Charles Robert Cockerell, a distinguished British neoclassical architect, admired for his "bold deployment of the orders and the beauty of his [classical] detail,"[1] visited Sardis during two days in March 1812. He was twenty-four, and on a Grand Tour in Greece, Turkey, and Italy from 1811 to 1817. This handsome pencil sketch shows the three columns of the Temple preserved intact in 1812, down from the six recorded by Wood and Borra in 1750, and the five recorded by Peyssonnel, also in 1750 (a few months after Wood's visit), and Richard Chandler in 1764.[2] Cockerell's drawing, a view of the east end of the Temple, looking southwest, clearly shows columns 7 and 6, and a third column on the right, or north, of these, probably number 16 (see fig. 17). Considering the angle and proportion, one would have imagined the third column to be number 17, the column directly in front of the southeast anta; however, since this column did not stand after 1750 we are left to infer that it is number 16, in front of the northeast anta pier. It appears that Cockerell's sketch was made from a spot on the rising Acropolis slopes east of the Temple; thus he had a wide field of vision, which he focused on the three eminent columns, much like the telescopic lens of a modern camera. The note at the upper right comments that the columns resemble those he saw in Athens in color, with blue streaks in them, but the capitals are "highly colored"—perhaps alluding to the strikingly rich yellow ocher hue of the capitals due to peculiar weathering conditions.

The Cockerell drawing, however, is inconsistent with his later published description of the Temple. Appearing as a quotation in a footnote of W. M. Leake's *Journal of a Tour in Asia Minor*, published in 1824, Cockerell asserted that "two columns of the exterior order of the east front [columns number 6 and 7], and one column of the portico of the pronaus [number 16], are still standing, with their capitals: the two former still support the stone of the architrave, which stretched from the centre of one column to the centre of the other."[3] In a simple sketch-elevation of the Temple's east front, published by Leake,[4] this architrave is shown in situ in a tentative way, and probably "as if restored." Our drawing has no architrave carried by any columns. Furthermore, none of the travelers who were in Sardis before Cockerell mention an architrave supported by the columns of the front row or include it in their drawings—for example, the Borra drawing, which shows remarkable detail and includes the architrave supported by porch columns 10 and 16. Cockerell probably did see this architrave on the ground close to columns 6 and 7 (a fully preserved architrave was found in this location by Butler), measured it, and identified its position correctly as having spanned these columns, and then he included it in a "restored elevation." But, in the note he wrote to Leake ten or twelve years after his visit to the Temple, he described it as if the architrave were in position. His fine drawing, always a better representative of an architect's ideas than his words, is characteristically correct.

Did the massive columns and handsome capitals of the Temple of Artemis serve as models, directly or indirectly, for Cockerell's later work? There is little question that the grand scale and exuberant decoration of the Ionic monuments of Asia Minor impressed the young architect and influenced his early work in a way that the more austere and small-scaled examples from Greece did not. The Ionic order of the pedimented portico of the Hanover Chapel in London, 1821, was directly inspired by a mixture of Anatolian models, such as the Temple of Athena in Priene and the Temple of Apollo in Didyma, but more specifically Sardis is singled out by Cockerell himself as the outstanding example in his diary entry for 29 April 1821: "Upon the chapel New Street [i.e., the Hanover Chapel, London; no longer extant] ... hit upon the double pilaster to carry tower & Portico ... chose Asiatic Ionic not yet seen—the cap[ital]s of Sardis...."[5]   FKY

1. Watkin 1982, 429.
2. Chandler 1775, 256.
3. Leake 1824, 342.
4. Leake 1824, 345.
5. Watkin 1974, 139.

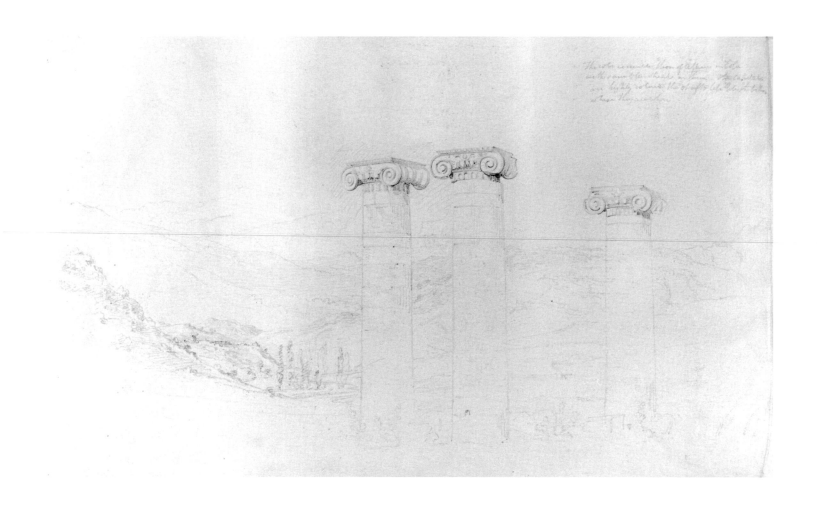

6

"THE ACROPOLIS OF SARDIS"

Thomas Allom (British, 1804–1872), c. 1838

Etching with hand-coloring on wove paper

21.4 × 28 cm (8⅜ × 11 in.)

Anonymous Loan

Published in Allom 1838, pl. 66; Vann 1989, fig. 13.

This etching shows a view of the site looking east, with the Pactolus Stream in the middle ground, Mt. Tmolus at right. Labels below the picture identify the Palace of Croesus (a common nineteenth-century name, not taken seriously by all those who used it, for the Roman Bath-Gymnasium Complex), Church of Panagia (probably Building D, identified by Auguste Choisy as a Church of St. George),[1] and Theater.

Thomas Allom was an architect and an artist. He designed buildings in and near London and Essex, and the layout of streets and parks in part of London (Ladbrook Grove); he illustrated topographical books on England, Scotland, France, and China, as well as on Constantinople and Asia Minor.[2] CHG

1. Choisy 1883, 160.
2. Radford 1885; Ware 1967.

7

SARDIS, VIEW OF THE SITE LOOKING
SOUTH

Thomas Allom, 1830s?

Etching with hand-coloring on wove paper

26.5 × 36.2 cm (10⅜ × 14¼ in.)

Anonymous Loan

At left appears Building C, a Roman building identified by Auguste Choisy as a
Church of St. John;[1] by others in recent
years as a basilica or another public bath.
Behind, at a higher level, is Building D, a
Late Roman or Byzantine building with
piers faced with spolia from older buildings, which was identified by Choisy as a
Church of St. George; and further behind,
on the lower slopes of the Acropolis, the
ancient Theater (see cats. 43, 44).

The water in the foreground is not a
feature of the present landscape. It could
be a fantasy of the artist, introduced to
make the view more picturesque, like some
of the ruins in the middle ground at right,
for which there is no evidence. More plausibly, however, the water is a feature of the
nineteenth-century landscape that no
longer exists. A millrace, which in the
nineteenth and twentieth centuries drew
water from a stream on the east side of the
Acropolis (today called Tabak çayı) and
serviced a modern mill just north of Building D, continued north from the mill and
seems to have passed between Mounds 2
and 3 into the Hermus River Valley. A
thick alluvial deposit north of Building
C—left foreground in the picture—indicates the existence there in recent centuries
of standing water, which could have been
introduced by the millrace. The foreground of Thomas Allom's picture should
be near the space between Mounds 2 and
3, and the water could represent water of
the race (mounds and buildings appear in
cats. 43, 44, 46).   CHG

1. Choisy 1883, 161.

8

TOMB OF KING ALYATTES OF LYDIA:
PLAN AND RESTORED ELEVATION,
FROM OLFERS 1859, PLS. II, III
(DETAILS OF EACH PLATE)

A. Schütze after a drawing by E. Ernstmann, c. 1858
or a few years earlier

Lithograph on wove paper

28.5 × 23 cm (11⅛ × 9⅛ in.) and 27.8 × 22.1 cm
(11 × 8¾ in.), sheets

Private Collection and President and Fellows of Harvard College/Harvard College Libraries, Arc 530.2

King Alyattes (reigned c. 610–560 B.C.) was the father of Croesus, the last king of Lydia (reigned c. 560–540s B.C.). Alyattes' reign was remembered by Greek writers for warfare against the Cimmerians, nomadic invaders from south Russia whom he succeeded in driving from Anatolia, and against the Greek cities of Smyrna, Clazomenae, and Miletus. Archaeologists have identified remains of his siege mound and destruction at Smyrna (Turkish Bayraklı, north of modern Izmir), and of one of two temples of Athena that he had built near Miletus, at Assesos, to atone for his destruction of her temple there during his raid on Milesian territory.

The tumulus of Alyattes was described by Herodotus (*History*, 1.9) as

the greatest work of man by far, saving the works in Egypt and in Babylon . . . the foundation whereof is of great stones and the rest of the tomb an heap of earth. This was wrought by the tradesmen and the craftsmen and the harlots. And upon the tomb there were landmarks even unto my day, five in number, with writings graven on them declaring what portions each of them had wrought; and when they were measured, it appeared that the share of the harlots was the greatest. . . . Now the circuit of the tomb is six stades and two plethra, and the breadth thirteen plethra. . . . The tomb is 1,280 yards in circumference; its breadth is 440 yards.[1]

The largest tumulus in the cemetery at Bin Tepe (called Koca Mutaf Tepe—"great sack hill"—in modern times) has a base diameter of more than 355 meters and a huge stone marker of "phallic" type (diameter 2.80 m; height 2.15 m) on its summit; at its base the tumulus is reported (by Spiegelthal) to have a stone curb wall or *crepis* of masonry with a maximum height of 18 meters. The estimated original base circumference of Koca Mutaf Tepe (today expanded as a result of erosion deposit) of 1115.33 meters is close to the circuit given by Herodotus, if his figures were calculated according to the Ionic foot of the Classical period (0.294 m): 1117.20.[2] Koca Mutaf Tepe was identified with the tomb of Alyattes by Robert Wood in 1750 and by Anton von Prokesch (later Anton Prokesch von Osten) in 1824; since the publication of von Prokesch's account in 1837, the identification has generally been accepted. In 1854 the tumulus was explored by the Prussian consul in Smyrna, Ludwig Peter Spiegelthal (1823–1900). He drove a tunnel into the south side of the tumulus and encountered a network of ancient tunnels, probably dug by grave robbers in Roman times. One of those tunnels led to a burial chamber: although its size is modest (the interior space measures only 3.32 by 2.27 meters and 2.33 meters high), its large and beautifully fitted and finished blocks of marble and limestone impress all who see them (fig. 5). Of funeral offerings only fragments of ordinary ceramic cups and unguent containers of pottery (*lydions*) and stone (*alabastra*) were recovered.[3]

A lively account of the chamber was written in 1881 or '82 by Francis H. Bacon (1856–1940; subsequently excavator of Assos, in the Troad, for the Archaeological Institute of America), in a letter to his architecture teacher at M.I.T., William R. Ware.

On the way to the mound Ali [Bacon's servant and guide] had been telling me stories of how there were always wolves or hyaenas in the tunnel . . . and tried to dissuade me from entering; but I had brought some candles with me for this very purpose and insisted on going in! . . . As we came up some buzzards fluttered off a dead, half-eaten horse, which lay across the mouth of the tunnel, and there were some bones inside. So there was probably some truth in the wolf story. Ali went ahead with cocked revolver ready to dose the first hyaena who should oppose American progress! I followed with my candle, and another Zaptieh [gendarme] was coming behind me with his revolver cocked, but I objected! . . . We came to the sepulchral chamber, and I have never seen a more impressive sight in my life than after that long clay tunnel to come suddenly on the beautifully fitted marble blocks, glistening by the light of our candles; and black as ink on top of the white roof slabs still lay the debris of the funeral pyre, charcoal and ashes! Then to think that there once lay the father of Croesus! Dramatic! wasn't it? Brigands outside; hyaenas in; sputtering candles; dead Lydian kings! . . . The masonry is superb! It made one's architectural blood tingle to see such enormous blocks cut so true and square, the joints very close and, of course, laid entirely without mortar in the best Greek fashion. Before leaving I stuck my visiting card in a crack in order to be polite to Alyattes, and crawled back through the passage, and came out looking like a chimney sweep, covered with perspiration, candle grease and clay, but happy![4]

The Harvard-Cornell Expedition explored the tumulus and its chamber on several occasions in 1962 and later years. The chamber and "phallic" marker on the summit were drawn and photographed, more pottery recovered from the chamber, and excavation outside the tumulus exposed traces of what may be a *crepis* wall.[5]

This plan and restored elevation were made for the publication of J. F. M. von Olfers, general director of the Berlin Museums, who became acquainted with Spiegelthal's excavation through Alexander von Humboldt (1769–1859), Spiegelthal's correspondent and Olfers's patron; Olfers never visited Sardis or Bin Tepe. Finished drawings or sketches from which the lithographs are derived have not been found. The Harvard University Library copy (Arc 530.2) contains contemporaneous marginal comments by an unidentified German intellectual who was familiar with sources of financial support for Spiegelthal's excavations. CHG

1. Translated by J. Enoch Powell (1949).
2. Ratté 1989, 7.
3. Olfers 1859, pl. V.
4. Letter of 1 June 1882, private collection.
5. Ratté 1989, 7–9, 157–62; Greenewalt, Ratté, and Rautman 1995, 22–24.

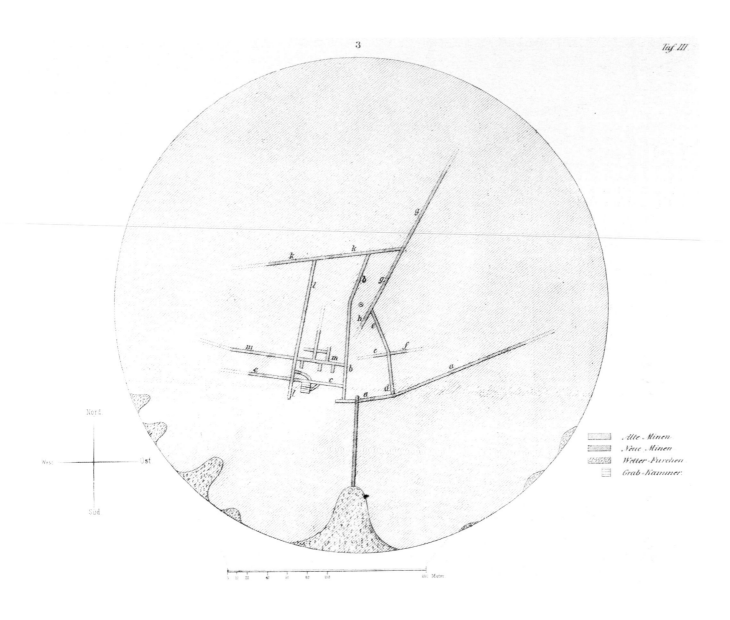

Nord

West ——— Ost

Süd

Alte Minen
Neue Minen
Wetter-Furchen
Grab-Kammer

0 10 20 40 60 80 100 — 200 Meter

4

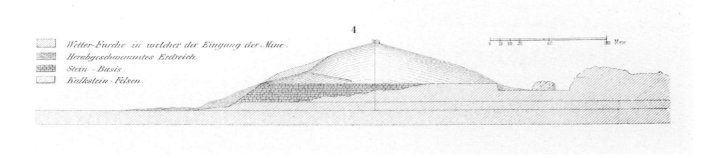

Wetter-Furche in welcher der Eingang der Mine.
Herabgeschwemmtes Erdreich.
Stein-Basis.
Kalkstein-Felsen.

0 10 20 30 60 — 100 Meter

Fig. 16. State plan of a Late Roman house, detail of rooms with walls of mortared rubble, floor of marble flagstone paving (left) and mosaic (center). These are rooms L, R, and T in cat. 17.

Paula B. Craft, 1997; Brian E. Jan, 1998; Jennifer K. Lathrop, 1999; black ink with traces of graphite on Mylar. Archaeological Exploration of Sardis, MMS-104, detail.

Crisp Lines

Philip T. Stinson

"Crisp Lines" refers to the tradition of using hard, fine lines for the recording of archaeological sites that developed in the nineteenth century when archaeological methods became more systematic and scientific. Measuring techniques and graphic conventions were adopted from the professions of architecture and civil engineering. Young practicing architects or students enrolled in architecture schools have created the majority of drawings done by the current Sardis excavation team. The first associate director of the Harvard-Cornell Expedition, A. Henry Detweiler (1906–1970), professor of architecture at Cornell University, had extensive excavation experience in the Near East and strongly believed that the education of practicing architects should include exposure to the architecture of Greece and Rome. This tradition continues today.

Measuring, conventions, and drawing types

An archaeological drawing at Sardis, whether it be of an excavation trench or of an unexcavated building, typically begins by utilizing various surveying and measuring techniques to establish the limiting lines of the subject matter on a sheet of graph paper. Before the development of electronic surveying (see "Infinite Points"), this part of the process was the most cumbersome and time consuming. The majority of the recording done at Sardis before the 1990s involved measuring over short distances and could be done with an optical transit or an alidade (cat. 9A). Like the optical transit, the alidade operated on principles of angle measurement with an optical scope, but, through an ingenious system employing the optical scope mounted on a leveled drawing tabletop called a plane table, it did not require complex mathematics. With the coming of digital surveying in the 1980s and 1990s, the electronic transit, or total station, replaced these instruments. As with the old system, however, all drawings still require several reliable benchmarks whose coordinates and elevations within the overall grid system are known. Coordinates on a two-dimensional grid with 0/0 at an arbitrary permanent point, plus elevations above sea level or an arbitrary 0, allow all objects, be they buildings or potsherds, to be precisely located in space and in relationship to one another. Major grid points are depicted on the plan drawings as small crosses along the margins (e.g., cats. 11–13, and see discussion of the Master Urban Plan, cat. 44). All measurements on the drawings are in meters, and the excavation works exclusively in the metric system.

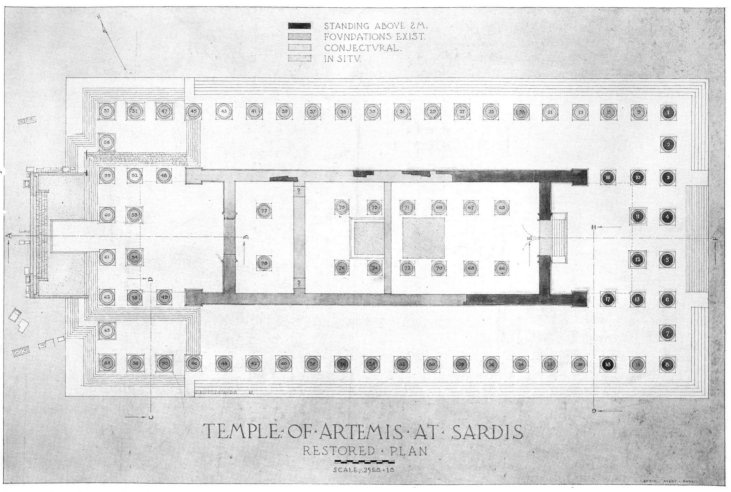

TEMPLE·OF·ARTEMIS·AT·SARDIS
RESTORED·PLAN
SCALE: 25 M. = 1 M.

Fig. 17. Butler's schematic plan of the Temple of Artemis showing building phases, column numbers, and restorations (Butler 1925, Text, pl. A).

Edwin Avery Park, before 1923.

The numbering system for columns devised by Bouverie and developed by Butler continues to be used by the current excavation. Exterior columns were numbered in rows from north to south, beginning at the east end and ending at the west; interior columns were numbered in continuation of that series, again from north to south and east to west. Surviving column capitals, all but two of which had fallen and become disassociated from their shafts by about 1825, were given letters.

The drawing itself is created by taking many individual measurements on the corners and edges of the subject matter and recording them on the graph paper. The measurements establish the relationship of the point in question to the overall site grid, and the points are then plotted on graph paper, typically reduced at a scale appropriate for the purpose of the drawing (cats. 9B, 15). As a rule of thumb, plans of excavation trenches are usually drawn at a scale of 1:50, that is, one meter on the drawing equals fifty meters in reality. The lines of the drawing on the graph paper are sketched in lightly at first; they are made darker with increased pressure on the pencil only after additional rounds of measuring and checking for mistakes. Because excavated architectural features are typically not preserved well, and also because they are often constructed of irregularly shaped materials such as field stones, straight lines are rare in archaeological recording. Aside from Lydian ashlar masonry, on drawings at Sardis straight lines are limited to the finely drafted edges of marble architecture from the Hellenistic and Roman periods. Completed field drawings are often inked in preparation for publication by overlaying them with vellum or Mylar and tracing over them with ink pens of various line weights. The graphic conventions consist mainly of thick lines to define the edges of walls, thin lines for cracks and fine details, and dots for mortar. The line work must be crisp and consistent, but should be drawn in such a way as to convey the appropriate level of preservation. For example, complete and cracked marble flagstone paving on the floor of a Roman house is drawn with both straight and irregular lines (fig. 16). Additions and corrections are often made to existing drawings as excavation sectors expand from year to year (cat. 11). Consequently, it is important to respect the established graphic conventions. Architects must stifle their individual drafting style in favor of an agreed-upon conventional one, although personal style and the possibility of whimsy are allowed in reconstruction drawings, especially in those intended for internal use only, such as preliminary sketch reconstructions (cats. 29, 36). With this said, personal style often shows through, as seen in many of these drawings. The drawings come to be signed with initials of the architects or archaeologists who were involved in making either the field drawing, the final ink drawing, or both. Ideally, the person who made the field drawing would ink it as well.

Several types of drawings are useful in archaeological recording. Plans, sections, and elevations are the most common. The general purpose of a plan is to communicate the structure or arrangement of a building or the spatial relationship between buildings and other archaeological features. A state plan conveys the state of preservation of an excavated structure or structures (cat. 24). Phase plans, which show groups of features associated by date or architectural organization, are often necessary to fully articulate the state of preservation in graphic terms (cats. 11–13). However, the separation of features associated by common period or architectural organization on distinct drawings is not always desirable. It is also important to understand the features of various epochs, remarkable or not, in relation to one another. To solve this problem, light lines—ghostlines—can be used to delineate features from earlier or later periods on the same drawing (cats. 11–13). This convention presupposes that other plans will be needed to fully understand the drawing. For instance, not even an experienced archaeologist would know what to make of the ghostline of the Lydian city wall as depicted on the mosaic and colonnade drawings (cats. 12, 13) without the help of the state plan of Lydian features (cat. 11). A composite plan collapses the information of distinct phase plans into one drawing with multiple superimposed phases (cat. 10). The composite plan is similar to the state plan, because the

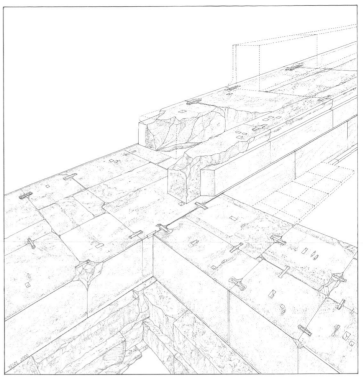

Fig. 18. Isometric view of connection of north cella wall and west crosswall of Temple of Artemis, looking northeast.

Fikret K. Yegül, 2000, black ink on Mylar. Archaeological Exploration of Sardis, AT-2000.8.

totality of phases is represented; but in a composite plan, features of disparate phases are often graphically schematized in order to clearly distinguish them from one another. Graphic conventions such as dashed lines and shading are used to prudently restore the traces of walls or features that are known to lie beneath others. The intent is to bring the whole into visual harmony without attracting undue attention to any one phase with extraneous details that would be more appropriately represented on a state plan. Consequently, composite plans hint at reuse and adaptation, information that is otherwise difficult to communicate graphically. Archaeologists invented another favorite, the findspot plan, to record the relationships of excavated objects, such as cooking pots or loom weights, to one another and to their architectural environment (cat. 14).

Elevation drawings record the front, side, or rear of a structure. Section drawings also cut through a feature while "looking" one direction or another, and often illustrate how a structure was constructed, or conversely, how it was destroyed. For instance, section drawings cutting through the

Fig. 19. Fikret Yegül on scaffolding drawing a capital of the Temple of Artemis (1992).

projection. Both types of drawings require an accurate plan drawing as the basis. The lines establishing the length and width in an isometric are drawn 30/30 degrees, respectively, from the bottom edge of the drafting table (the T-square or parallel bar), while the axonometric is a 45/45 or 30/60 projection. Consequently, the isometric is more difficult to draw because it requires the plan, which is the basis for the drawing, to be redrawn completely (cat. 17). The axono-metric is easier to produce, because the existing plan can simply be rotated and walls and three-dimensional features projected up from it by tracing over it with a sheet of Mylar or paper (fig. 33). These drawings are useful to simulate a bird's-eye view. More complex perspective drawings are usually saved for attempts at reconstructing the third dimension based on archaeological evidence (see "Dashed Lines"). Three-dimensional drawings are today created at least in part with the help of a computer (cat. 50).

Recording the Temple of Artemis

Drawings in the exhibition of the Temple of Artemis provide examples of several different approaches to graphic recording. As a group they serve as evidence of how attitudes toward antiquity have changed in culture and in the field of archaeology from the mid-eighteenth century to the present day. The architect for Robert Wood, Giovanni Battista Borra, created the earliest surviving drawings of the Temple in 1750 (see "Brush Strokes"). Borra seems to have been interested in drawing exactly what he saw, and he recorded the ruins of the Temple within their majestic topographical setting as accurately as he could, given his short stay at the site and the means available (cat. 4).

The drawings of the Temple by the Butler Expedition after they completely cleared it from 1910 to 1914 serve as the first archaeological publication of the monument. Because of Turkey's involvement in World War I, Howard Crosby Butler was forced to suspend excavations in 1914. He returned in 1922 to assess the possibility of reopening excavations, but became ill on his trip home and died in Paris. The set of drawings that was eventually published included two full plans of the Temple—a detailed ink-line state plan at 1:200, and a schematic state plan with restorations at 1:400 (fig. 17)—as well as several restored elevations and sections, and many restored drawings of the Temple's Ionic ornament. Butler's architects were well-trained draftsmen, but they tended in their drawings to restore

well-preserved remains of the colossal Lydian mudbrick city wall show the profile of the wall as well as the debris that fell from it when it was partially burned and destroyed by the forces of Cyrus during the Persian sack of Sardis in the 540s B.C. (cat. 16).

Plans, elevations, and sections are two-dimensional drawings, and thus are limited to showing features at some level of abstraction. Drawings of physical remains in three dimensions can be helpful companions to two-dimensional representations and photographs. Simple three-dimensional drawings can be created by projecting lines up from a ground plan, either through an isometric or an axonometric more than is common today. In fact, most of the drawings in Butler's publication are restorations that do not show exactly what is preserved and what is restored or reconstructed. This drawing technique results from the Beaux-Arts tradition, which was influential in the architecture schools of America in the early twentieth century.

Fikret K. Yegül's current project, begun in 1987, aims to record, for the first time, the Temple's preserved standing remains and unfinished details in their entirety. For instance, he draws all the ornamental elements but gives equal attention to the building's more mundane features. Yegül's plan of the Temple is at 1:20 scale, ten times the scale of Butler's largest plan. According to Yegül, the Butler team never did a 1:20 scale plan of the Temple because that level of accuracy was not needed for their research. Because of its large scale, the new plan includes a host of construction features—the "guts" of the building—such as clamp and dowel holes for fastening the marble blocks together and incised setting lines for aligning blocks against one another (cat. 24). Yegül's drawings also painstakingly record the surface texture of the blocks, including chisel marks left by the ancient masons' tools that are still visible as well as all the cracks and fissures in the marble. Three-dimensional drawings further illustrate how the Temple was constructed, and the state it survives in today (fig. 18). In 1994 Yegül erected scaffolding around each of the two "sentries" of the Temple in order to study and draw the only Ionic capitals that remain in their original positions (fig. 19; cats. 23, 26). This was not possible previously, although Lansing C. Holden, one of Butler's architects in 1922, did hoist himself up to the top of one of the capitals using rope and tackle (cat. 22).

ALIDADE (PLANE TABLE INSTRUMENT)

Gurley Engineering Instruments, Troy, N.Y.

Lacquered and silvered brass, aluminum, glass, and steel

10.5 × 28.8 × 10 cm (5 × 12 × 4 in.)

Archaeological Exploration of Sardis

9B

PLANE TABLE SHEET FOR MMS/N-14A: LYDIAN FEATURES PLAN, 1:50

Thomas N. Howe, 1982

Black and blue ink and graphite on three sheets of wove graph paper

53 × 67.9 cm (20⅞ × 26¾ in.)

Archaeological Exploration of Sardis

A: The alidade is a telescopic instrument that is set up on a leveled drawing board or plane table and swivels around a fixed axis. It works in essentially the same way that other surveying instruments work: it determines the distance and direction between the instrument and the object it is measuring. The architect pins the axis of the telescope to the center of the board. He or she then sights through the telescope to the object being measured; this establishes the direction. He then measures the distance with a tape measure from the alidade to the object (fig. 20). The distance is drawn to scale as a line from the axis of the alidade along the ruler on its side. The endpoint of the line then locates the object on the drawing. These radial lines that locate measured points are visible on the field sheet under the instrument. The alidade therefore avoids the difficulties of triangulation and complex trigonometry that surveying with a transit requires, but it is only appropriate for surveying over very short distances and is generally not as accurate as a transit. NDC

B: The drawing shown in the photograph was the original field sheet for the plan of the gate passage in the Lydian city wall, cat. 11, but it was drawn in the early 1980s before the gate passage was identified as such. The faint straight lines that radiate from the numerous benchmarks indicate that the limiting lines of the drawing were created with an alidade mounted on a leveled plane table. Some features were also drawn on the field sheet using a simpler triangulation method that required taped measurements and a beam compass. The graphic conventions illustrate the basic principles of archaeological field drawing. The sheet also shows the wear and tear of several years of use and reuse at Sardis. Several "final drawings" of the gate passage have been made over the years, the latest being the one shown in cat. 11. Previous versions were rendered obsolete as excavations expanded and as the aims and purposes of the drawing changed. This field sheet, however, has been continually referenced for each subsequent retracing, which largely accounts for its dingy appearance. Some of the pencil lines were hastily inked with heavy black lines from a felt-tip pen at some point, presumably because the pencil lines were not discernible through the sheet of Mylar used for an ink tracing. The grid paper was also recently nibbled at by a crafty mouse, who found it very useful for the construction of a nest to raise her young ones in the back of the architects' drafting supply cabinet in the basement of the Expedition house in Turkey. PTS

Fig. 20. Brian Percival and Richard Penner using plane table and alidade (1968).

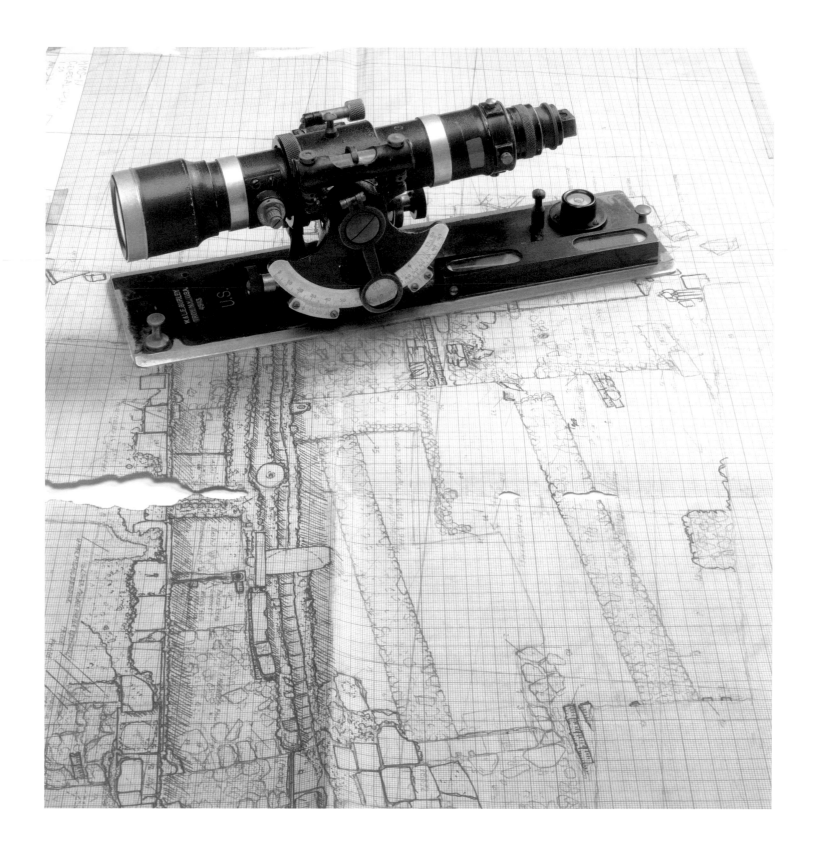

10

Sectors MMS, MMS/N, MMS/S: Composite features plan of three sectors of monumental mudbrick structure (Lydian city wall)

Philip T. Stinson, Nicholas D. Cahill,
James M. Toris, 2003

Computer-generated drawing

Archaeological Exploration of Sardis, MMS-82A

This composite plan depicts the excavated remains of the Lydian city wall of the mid-sixth century B.C. and, one thousand years later, a Late Roman porticoed street and houses of the fourth to seventh century A.D. The Roman houses were built on top of the ruins of the Lydian city wall, so they appear on the uppermost layer in the drawing. Unlike the phase plans in cats. 11–13, this plan is deliberately schematic, omitting details of architecture and construction to show the more general relations between features.

Chronological phases are shown in different colors: red for Roman remains, blue for material of the Persian period, and purple and green for different features of the Lydian period. The darker shades are used for excavated remains; restored areas are depicted in lighter shades of the same colors. Such a plan cannot show how high features are standing or the vertical relations between them, although these are often very important. Sections, isometric and axonometric views, and sketches—such as cats. 16, 17, 29, 30—add this important third dimension.

The drawing is based on a total station survey (fig. 21) of all the excavated remains; it replaces an earlier ink drawing on Mylar that was created with traditional surveying techniques. It is useful for understanding several other drawings in the exhibition: cats. 11–13, 17, and 29–34.   PTS, NDC

Fig. 21. Philip Stinson and Brian Jan surveying with total station (1998).

Roman Bath-Gymnasium Complex

Lydian City Wall

S 0

Gate Blockage

Gate Passage

Former Izmir-Ankara Highway

S 40

Glacis

S 60

S 80

Late Roman Houses

Persian Wall

Lydian City Wall

S 100

S 120

S 140

S 160

E 90

E 130

E 150

E 170

0 1 3 5   10   20m.

Sectors: MMS, MMS-North, MMS-South
Composite Features Plan

PTS, JMT 1999-2003

Key

Trench Line

Roman Features

Persian Features

Lydian Features

Restored Lydian Features

Restored Glacis

Excavated Glacis Sloping Layers

Glacis Stone Retaining Wall

11

Sector MMS/N: Lydian features plan, 1:50

Troy D. Thompson, Susan M. Hickey, 1990; Philip T. Stinson, 1991; Philip T. Stinson, Kathryn A. Courteau, 1992; Philip T. Stinson, 1993, 1994; Julie Y. Chang, 1995; Philip T. Stinson, Zachary N. Hinchliffe, 1996; Brian F. Jan, 1998

Black ink with traces of graphite on Mylar

97.3 × 114.7 cm (38¼ × 45⅛ in.)

Archaeological Exploration of Sardis, MMS/N-14A

Published in Greenewalt, Ratté, and Rautman 1995, fig. 13; Greenewalt and Rautman 1998, fig. 15.

This is a phase plan—a plan showing the preserved remains of one building phase only (in this case, Lydian)—of a gate passage in the Lydian city wall. The plan also shows large blocking walls built after the partial destruction of the wall in the middle of the sixth century B.C., probably as a result of the siege and capture of Sardis by the Persians in the 540s B.C. Thin lines denote a Roman colonnaded avenue and plaza built over the top of the ruins of the city wall and gate passage one thousand years later, in the fifth century A.D.

For an original field sheet, one of many that was used to compose this ink drawing, see cat. 9B. For three-dimensional reconstruction views of the gate passage, see cats. 32–34. For a schematic composite plan, see cat. 10; cats. 12 and 13 show later phases of this same sector.   PTS

E 130

E 140

E 150

E 160

S 00

OCCUPATION
SURFACE

COBBLE PAVINGS

COBBLE PAVINGS

COBBLE PAVINGS

COBBLE PAVINGS

COBBLE
PAVING

COBBLE
PAVING

COBBLE PAVINGS

S 30

0 1   3   5   10m

MMS-N:
LYDIAN FEATURES PLAN

TDT, SMH   1990   JYC   1995
        PTS   1991   PTS, ZNH   1996
KAC, PTS   1992   BEJ   1998
        PTS   1993
        PTS   1994

12

Sector MMS/N: Upper mosaic features plan, 1:50

Philip T. Stinson, 1991, 1992, 1993, 1994;
Zachary N. Hinchliffe, 1996

Black ink with traces of graphite on Mylar

98.2 × 126.7 cm (38⅝ × 49¾ in.)

Archaeological Exploration of Sardis, MMS/N-21

Published in Greenewalt, Ratté, and Rautman 1994,
fig. 4; Greenewalt, Ratté, and Rautman 1995, fig. 5;
Greenewalt and Rautman 1998, fig. 3.

This phase plan depicts the upper mosaic of an ambulatory space with two rows of columns, which was originally inside a covered portico and looked out onto a large plaza or street paved in white marble slabs. The function of the ambulatory space is unknown. It may have simply been a covered sidewalk, but it is also conceivable that commercial activities took place here. When this mosaic was partially removed in the hopes of revealing Lydian levels, the excavators discovered another mosaic beneath it (cat. 13). On this drawing and that of the lower level, the mosaics were drawn with thin black lines that depict only the geometric patterns. Subtle color changes were impossible to record at the scale of 1:50, and consequently, some drawings of details were made at a larger scale. Three-dimensional reconstruction views of the sequence of occupation in this area from Lydian to Late Roman times are shown in cats. 32–34. For a schematic composite plan, see cat. 10.   PTS

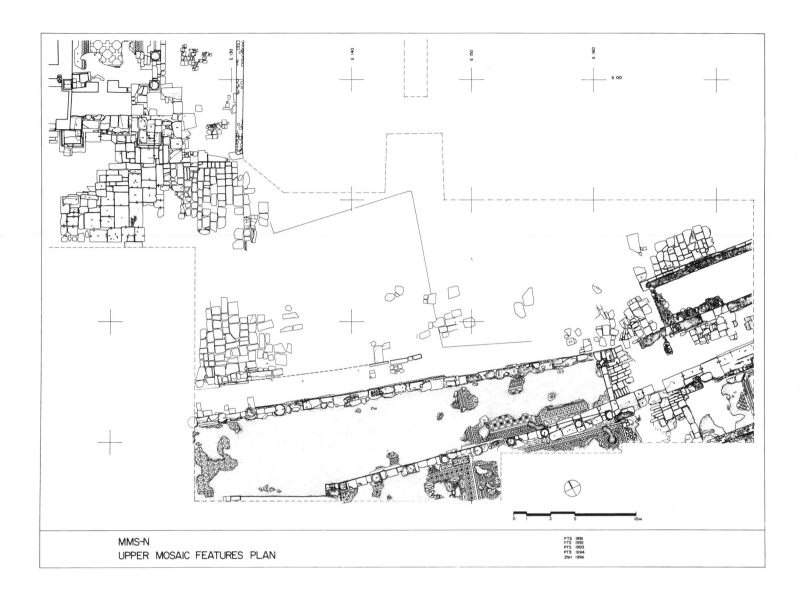

E 130 E 140 E 150 E 160

S 00

MMS-N
UPPER MOSAIC FEATURES PLAN

0 1 3 5 10m

PTS 1991
PTS 1992
PTS 1993
PTS 1994
ZNH 1996

13

Sector MMS/N: Lower mosaic features plan, 1:50

Troy D. Thompson, Philip T. Stinson, 1991;
Philip T. Stinson, 1992, 1993

Black ink with traces of graphite and purple
pencil on Mylar

98.1 × 111 cm (38⅜ × 43⅝ in.)

Archaeological Exploration of Sardis, MMS/N-22

Published in Greenewalt, Ratté, and Rautman 1994,
fig. 5.

This phase plan is of the lower mosaic of
an ambulatory space that was originally
inside a covered portico and looked out
onto a large plaza or street paved in white
marble slabs. The lower mosaic is approximately fifteen centimeters (about six in.)
below a later mosaic (see previous entry).
The drawing also shows the remains of the
white marble paving of a plaza or street to
the north. The lower mosaic inscription
(IN90.21) reads "The colonnaded street
was paved with mosaic and received all
the decoration when Flavius Archelaos,
companion of the first rank of his Serene
Highness, held the Office of Prefect." This
mosaic was lifted and placed in storage in
order to excavate the lower levels (see cat.
11 for the Lydian features found underneath). For a schematic composite plan,
see cat. 10.   PTS

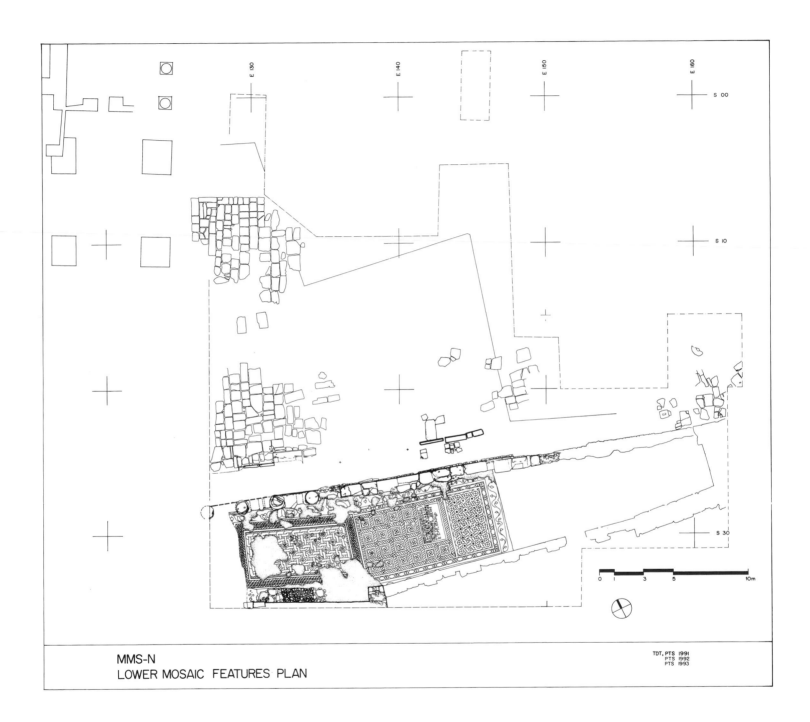

E 130 E 140 E 150 E 160

S 00

S 10

S 30

0 1   3   5   10m

MMS-N
LOWER MOSAIC FEATURES PLAN

TDT, PTS 1991
PTS 1992
PTS 1993

14

Sector MMS-I: Plan of Lydian houses and domestic assemblages

Nicholas D. Cahill, 1995–2003

Computer-generated drawing

Archaeological Exploration of Sardis, MMS-147

Published in Greenewalt, Ratté, and Rautman 1995, fig. 14; Cahill 2000, 176.

This findspot plan records parts of two Lydian houses. The houses were burned in the mid-sixth century B.C. in the cataclysm that also destroyed the fortification; they were then buried under the debris of the fortification and their own walls, preserving their walls and contents as a frozen moment of time (this same destruction debris is drawn in cat. 16). The plan shows both the architecture of the houses and the pottery and other objects smashed on their floors, as found during excavation. Unlike the Temple of Artemis and other buildings which can be drawn and redrawn over a period of time, artifacts must be recorded immediately upon excavation; once removed from the ground, the evidence of their original context is lost. This drawing is an essential record of the context of the hundreds of pots and other artifacts from these houses, and shows how different rooms and parts of rooms were used. The plan is a composite of drawings of the walls and other features made by the architects, field drawings by the archaeologists from four seasons of excavation (including cat. 15), and electronic surveys of the standing architecture.

Green indicates mudbrick preserved on stone socles. Where the mudbrick was not preserved (particularly on the east), the stones of the socle are drawn. Lighter green is used for reconstructed walls. Orange stippling is used for hearths. Different colors are used for different classes of artifacts: various shapes of pottery, metals, stone, foodstuffs, etc.

An earlier version of this plan was drawn on Mylar. After further excavation made updating the Mylar drawing impractical, this digital plan was created. Its digital format makes updating and modifying the drawing significantly easier than redrawing on a larger sheet of Mylar.   NDC

E 145   E 150   E 155

S 55

S 60

S 65

S 70

	Hearths
	Cooking vessels
	Table Pottery
	Grindstones
	Loomweights
	Iron, hardware
	Foodstuffs

MMS-I: Plan of Lydian Houses
and Domestic Assemblages

0   5 m.

MMS-147   NDC 1986-2003

15

FIELD SHEET FOR PLAN MMS-147, 1:10

Nicholas D. Cahill, 1986

Graphite and red ink on wove graph paper

56 × 75.8 cm (22 × 29¾ in.)

Archaeological Exploration of Sardis

This field sheet is one of a series that records the destruction debris in a room of a Lydian house and forms the basis for the final plan in cat. 14. As objects were identified in the field they were given numbers and noted on the plan; this makes it possible to identify exactly where each was found. These field numbers were not intended for publication, and so do not appear on the final plan, but together with other field notes and information they are an important part of the excavation's primary record. Elevations are shown, as conventionally at Sardis, prefixed with an asterisk. The grid shown on the plan, labeled with one-meter squares (1K, 2K, etc.) is purely arbitrary, set out with strings during excavation; the strings were later surveyed on the B-grid (shown in cat. 14; see cat. 44).   NDC

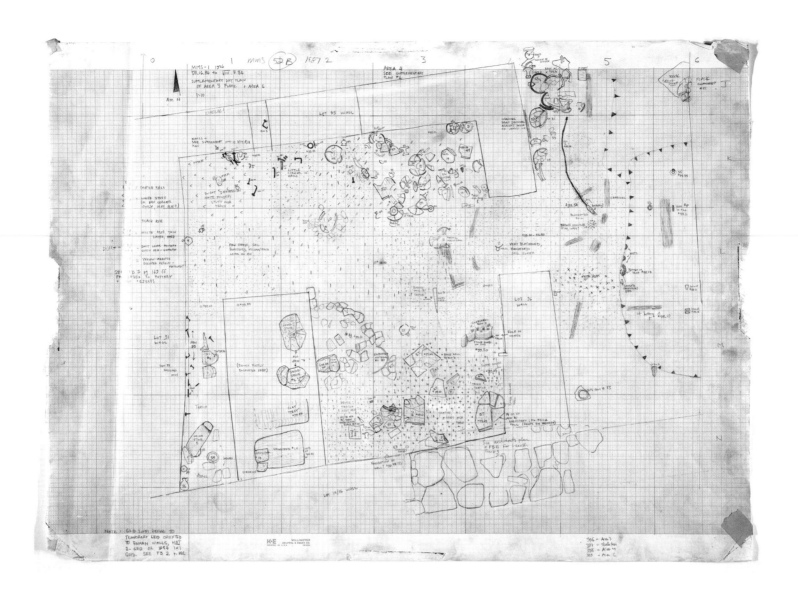

16

Sector MMS: Fallen brick and debris from Lydian colossal structure, looking south, 1:20

Christine M. Lindinger, 1984

Colored pencil and graphite on white wove paper

77 × 123.4 cm (30½ × 48¼ in.)

Archaeological Exploration of Sardis, MMS-32A

This section drawing looks south at the scarp of a deep excavation trench dug to expose the Lydian city wall (cf. fig. 22). On the right side of the drawing, the heavy line is a section cut through the wall face, which is not vertical but slightly sloped. At the left, a heavy line cuts through a house wall of the Lydian period (lower left in cat. 14). The colored rectangles between are a tumble of brick debris, the remains of the superstructure of the fortification wall, which must originally have been significantly higher than preserved today—more than fifteen meters in height, or about fifty feet. The mudbricks are of different colors—green, brown, purplish, and red—and the fortification wall must once have been brilliantly polychrome. The red bricks were semibaked, perhaps to make them more weatherproof.

The drawing shows more clearly than a photograph how the brick debris consists of layers of more and less complete bricks, with larger bricks and brick fragments concentrated on the left at the lower end of the slope. This is evidence that the wall was intentionally demolished and the brick debris dumped from the top of the wall. Found in the destruction debris and on the floors it covered were armor, weapons, and the skeletons of two young men, apparently soldiers. All this suggests a military destruction rather than a natural catastrophe. Pottery from the houses (see cat. 14) and other contexts associated with this layer dates to the middle of the sixth century B.C., leading to the identification of this destruction with the capture of Sardis by Cyrus of Persia in the 540s B.C. NDC

Fig. 22. South scarp of MMS-I with Adil Akça for scale (1996).

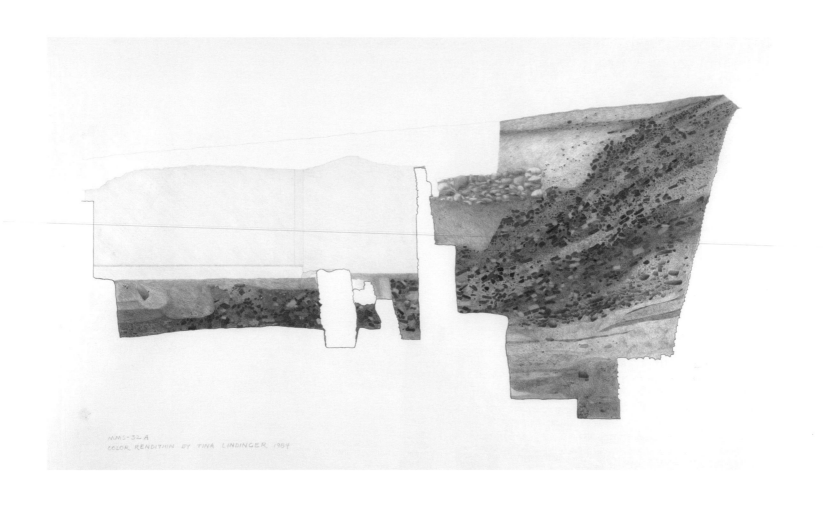

MMS-32 A
COLOR RENDITION BY TINA LINDINGER 1984

17

SECTOR MMS/S: LATE ROMAN
RESIDENTIAL UNITS, ISOMETRIC VIEW
LOOKING WEST, 1:75

Philip T. Stinson, 1998

Black ink with traces of graphite on Mylar

71.4 × 91.1 cm (28 × 36 in.)

Archaeological Exploration of Sardis, MMS-110

Published in Greenewalt 2000, fig. 2.

This isometric drawing illustrates a Late
Roman house in three dimensions, with
walls standing to their preserved heights.
The same house appears in plan in cat. 10
(lower half of the image) and in fig. 30
(most clearly at far right). The house had a
two-hundred-year history, in the fifth and
sixth centuries A.D. In its last major phase,
it had twelve ground-floor rooms (with a
total area of approx. 1300 square meters)
and an upper floor, reached by two stair-
cases. The function of a few spaces may be
tentatively identified. The one labeled D is
a triclinium (dining room); E an entrance
courtyard (with entrance from the colonnaded street to the north); F perhaps a
lower-level service vestibule, with its own
street entrance and connecting staircase to
A on the main floor; L another open court;
O a reception hall; and M and R contained latrines (but that of R, like a hearth
that it also contained, is a very late feature). O and R had mosaic pavings; D an
opus sectile paving (colorful marble slabs
cut and arranged in geometric configura-
tions) at the front of the dining platform;
E, L, and P marble flagstone paving; A, M,
and Q terracotta tile paving. D, E, O, and
R had painted and stuccoed wall decoration. Noteworthy contents, in addition to
pottery and coins, include a marble sigma
tabletop, found resting on the dining platform in D, and an assemblage of twenty-
one glass weights in N.[1] The house was
excavated over several seasons: 1979,
1991 (A), and 1995–98 (D–F, L–R, T).[2]

Figure 16 shows room R at center (with
its latrine recessed in the right-hand wall),
court L at left, and room T at right.
CHG, PTS

1. Fulghum and Heintz 1998.
2. Rautman in Greenewalt and Rautman 2000,
   646–55.

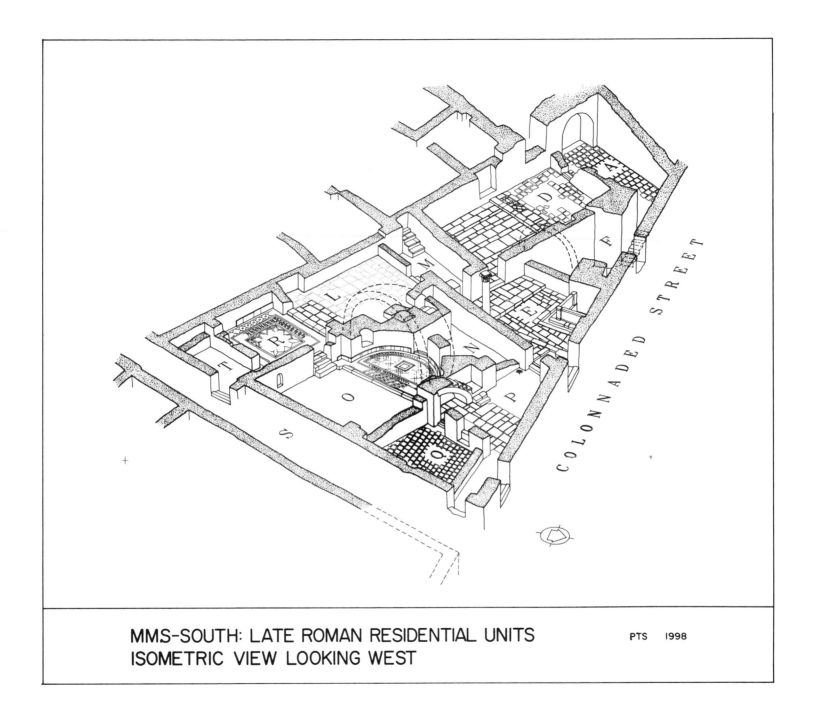

MMS-SOUTH: LATE ROMAN RESIDENTIAL UNITS
ISOMETRIC VIEW LOOKING WEST

PTS   1998

18

TEMPLE OF ARTEMIS: "CURTAIN WALL
IN CELLA," NORTH HALF OF CROSS-
WALL, FROM BUTLER EXPEDITION
ARCHITECTS' NOTEBOOK, P. 7, C. 1911

Graphite on wove paper in field book

11.9 × 19.5 cm (4¾ × 7¾ in.)

Department of Art and Archaeology,
Princeton University

"We discovered one entire course of well
fitted marble blocks extending from wall
to wall, which had constituted the foundations of a light wall or barrier dividing the
naos into a larger and a smaller compart-
ment."[1] With these words Butler described
the 0.90-meter-wide "crosswall" found
during the second Temple campaign in
1911. The wall was sketched in pencil, for
the first time, in the so-called Architects'
Notebook, an archaeological field book
for recording daily discoveries. We do not
know who made the measured sketch, but
it is likely that it was Charles Read, the assistant engineer that year and the draftsman for numerous drawings published in
the 1925 Atlas of Plates.[2]

The part covered by this field plan is a
fourteen-meter stretch of the crosswall
from the connection it makes with the
long north wall of the Temple (left) to
roughly the middle of foundation base 74
(or, 3.30 m short of the south wall, right).
Foundation base 73, fully sketched, is on
the lower left, or west (see fig. 17). No
north arrow is drawn, but east and west
are indicated by the letters E and W. The
sketch is clear, accurate, and includes written measurements, but is fairly rudimen-
tary; it is "measured," but not drawn to
any scale. The length and width of each
block are simply written on each one.
Overall dimensions that help to position
the new wall vis-à-vis the main walls of
the cella are entered briefly, such as "10.55
to fin. int. wall in situ" or "13.08 to wall
of opisthodomos." Construction features
and details, such as lewis holes, dowel
holes, or setting lines, are omitted; only
the connections of blocks to each other by
clamps are carefully indicated by simple

double lines. Perhaps the size and scale of
the notebook sketch was judged to be too
small to include more information (compare the relevant portion of the new 1:20
scale in cat. 24). No detailed levels—necessary to do a section or elevation—are included in the sketch plan, but short
descriptive statements record randomly
chosen relative heights: the top course of
the crosswall is identified as "1st course
below pavement," and it is given as 0.53
[m] in height. The two foundations for the
interior columns, 73 and 74, are simply
described as "lower than curtain wall,"
and the individual heights of their lower
projecting courses are noted. These heights
must have been simply measured by tape;
this is not a technical drawing whose levels
are determined by the use of the transit or
the dumpy level.

This measured sketch plan of the so-
called curtain wall in the cella, as well as
many others that must have been done in
the field during the 1910–14 excavation of
the building, must have been the primary
sources for the final 1:200 scale state plan
of the Temple published in the Atlas in
1925. Yet, this plan (the only one they did)
has no more detail than the quick sketches
in the Architects' Notebook. It is curious
that for all the monumental effort made to
excavate and study this great building and
its ornament, Butler must not have felt the
need to record its architecture and construction in any great detail. War was ap-
proaching, so perhaps he never had the
time, or maybe he merely did not believe
that such minute recording and examina-
tion of raw construction details, clamp
holes, lewis holes, and surface marks were
as important to the study and dating of the
Temple as its fine ornament and beautiful
capitals. That is why, recognizing the need
some eighty years later, we covered the
same ground as Butler's good draftsman,
but included far more detail in our state
plan drawn at 1:20, a scale ten times
larger than that of its precursor.   FKY

1. Butler 1922, 64.
2. The Atlas of Plates for Butler 1925 (*Sardis*, vol. 2,
   Architecture, part 1, *The Temple of Artemis*).

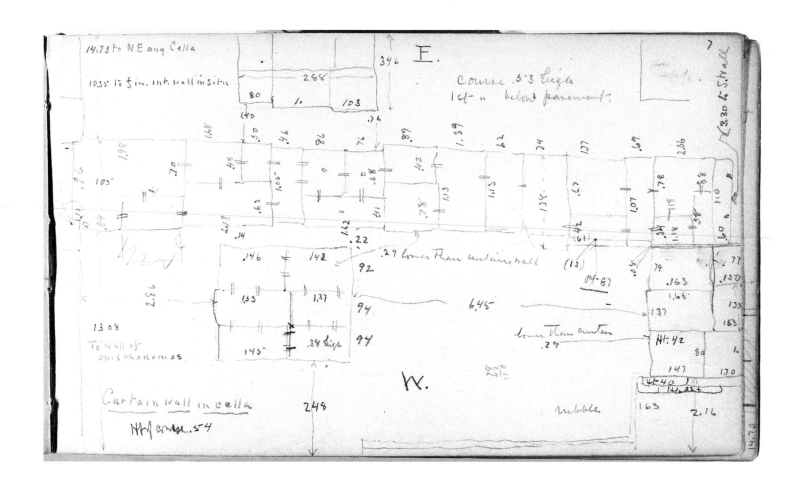

14.73 to N E ang Cella

10.35 to ƒ in. int. wall in situ

E.

346

Course .5·3 high
1 st " below pavement.

2.88

80   1.   103

1.40   .76

Curtain wall in cella

Ht of course .54

13.08
To wall of
opisthodomos

W.

248

.29 lower than curtain wall

(13)

6.45

rubble

lower than curtain
.29

Ht. 42

19A

TEMPLE OF ARTEMIS: PRELIMINARY
SKETCH OF CAPITAL D, 1:2

Graphite on wove paper

15.4 × 64 cm (6⅛ × 25⅛ in.)

Department of Art and Archaeology,
Princeton University

19B

TEMPLE OF ARTEMIS: PRELIMINARY
SKETCH OF CAPITAL D, 1:2

Graphite on wove paper

17.4 × 47.8 cm (6⅞ × 18¾ in.)

Department of Art and Archaeology,
Princeton University

In field recording practice, an overall drawing of a complex architectural ornament is normally created from or supplemented by various larger-scale, more detailed pencil sketches of some of its important components. In these "parts" drawings, lines are sharper and crisper as the draftsman focuses on a selected detail. Later, perhaps in the field but more often in the drafting room, individual components of these sketches are recomposed into one finished drawing. Neither of these sketches includes written measurements or a graphic scale, but they are drawn to the scale of 1:2. Although they are in pencil, both sketches are finely rendered, precise, and the same size as the final drawing of Butler capital D, which was then reduced by 50 percent (for a scale of 1:4) when published as plate XVII in the Expedition publication's Atlas of Plates (cat. 21). There is little question that they were done in Sardis in 1922, but they may be hard-line study versions of more informal, free-hand, dimensioned field sketches, now lost. They are somewhat modified but fairly exact representations of the published version (except that one, 19B, is reversed in the publication).

In the time-honored tradition of architects and artists, five separate ornamental details from capital D are randomly distributed across a sheet of tracing paper in 19A. The main sketch, occupying the left half of the paper, is a vertical section through the bottom of the bolster of the capital, shown in delicate pencil: the elevation view of the upward palmette located at the far channel of the volute; the reed growing out of an acanthus leaf curling upwards. Also on this sheet are a crisp detail of a single egg-and-dart from the abacus; a corner egg with its reversed palmette ornament; a partial rendition of a larger egg, which is, perhaps, the profile of the larger egg of the echinus; and a faint and tentative study of what appears to be a simplified acanthus leaf occupying a corner.

Sketch 19B shows the left half volute ornament of capital D (shown as right half in the Atlas plate). This drawing is, in fact, a partial field reconstruction: only the central rosette, the twisted acanthus stalks that start below it, and the small bellflowers that terminate the acanthus scroll above the volutes are preserved. Of the acanthus scroll nothing survives except a few stubs, and perhaps a ghostlike trace of its curling stalk, which might have been more visible in 1922 than it is now. In their reconstructions, the draftsmen used the better-preserved acanthus scroll motif from capitals A, E, and C as general models.[1] The last named (taken in 1922 to the Metropolitan Museum of Art in New York) was especially admired for the crisp beauty of its ornament, and it was drawn and reconstructed in beautiful Beaux-Arts style by Maitland Belknap and included as a pair of sepia-toned plates in Butler 1925 (Text, pls. B, C; see fig. 10).

The inclusion of one motif in 19B is intriguing: there is a downward bellflower with six petals emerging between the left and right curling stalks, a detail not preserved on capital D, or any other capital from the Temple. This motif is also not shown on the elevation/section mock-up

sketch of capital D (cat. 20), but does appear in the final version (cat. 21). On capital C this position is filled by a simple triangular leaf stub. Might Butler's talented draftsmen have seen something on the stone we now cannot make out, or did they simply admire the pair of exquisite bellflowers preserved at the ends of the acanthus ornament of capital D and decide to "reconstruct" this unique detail at an appropriate place on the capital?   FKY

1. Indicated by Gordon McCormick and Lansing C. Holden, Jr., in Butler 1925, Text, 145.

20

TEMPLE OF ARTEMIS: PREPARATORY
DRAWING OF CAPITAL D FOR PLATE
XVII IN BUTLER 1925, ATLAS,
APPROXIMATELY 1:4

Graphite on wove paper

50 × 74.7 cm (19½ × 29⅜ in.)

Department of Art and Archaeology,
Princeton University

(NOT IN THE EXHIBITION)

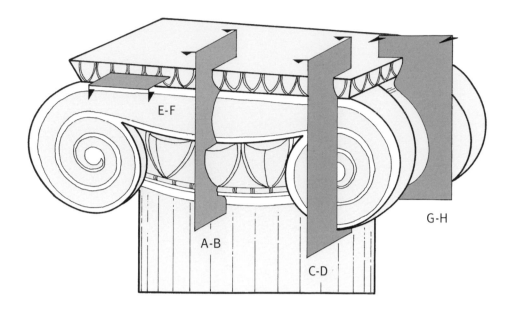

This composite drawing of capital D combines the right half in elevation and several vertical sections taken through the middle egg (labeled section A–B); the volute (section C–D); the middle of the bolster with the backside of the volute in elevation (section G–H); and a horizontal section of abacus showing egg-and-dart clusters (section E–F) (see fig. 23). There is also a short vertical section to show the volute band, but it was crossed out as if it were decided not to include this detail in the final version (cat. 21).

This drawing is a freehand layout sketch of capital D published as plate XVII (cat. 21) in the Atlas of Plates portion of the *Temple of Artemis* volume published in 1925. Indeed, the layout of the published version—which is actually based on other field sketches measured and drawn to scale, such as those illustrated in cat. 19—follows this sketch almost exactly. The upper left label "Sardis Vol. II" identifies the drawing, as does the handwritten inscription above: "For Cap G Plate the arrangement & drawings will be the same as this plate. Total No. of Plates for Cap D = 2, for Cap G = 1." This, indeed, is correct; there is a second plate (plate XVIII) for capital D in the Atlas while capital G is represented by one plate only.

The sketch is not dated or signed by its draftsman. However, it was almost certainly made in 1922 when Lansing C. Holden, Jr., and Gordon McCormick, supervised by H. C. Butler, undertook a special trip to Sardis for further study of the capitals (see cat. 22). The draftsman of this sketch is probably Gordon McCormick, since the finished drawings of

capital D and capital G in the Atlas are both signed by him, while his architect companion Lansing Holden signed the three plates representing capital E.

One of the best-preserved capitals from the Temple (along with capital C now in the Metropolitan Museum of Art, New York), capital D is displayed on top of the south side base 34, on site, where Butler had placed it in 1912. Almost identical in dimensions to capitals C and G, it belongs to the "small" group of Sardis capitals, which are roughly 12 percent smaller than capitals E and F, and 20 percent smaller than capitals A and B. It has recently been assigned to a middle position in the *pronaos* porch, either on the slender, fluted columns on pedestal bases (numbers 11, 12), or their western counterparts (53, 54).
FKY

Fig. 23. Drawing to indicate sections shown in Butler capital drawings.

James M. Toris, 2003. Archaeological Exploration of Sardis, AT-121.

PLATE XXXI

Note { For Cap G. Plate the arrangement & drawings will be the same
{ as this plate.
{ Total N°. of Plates for Cap D = 2, for Cap G = 1

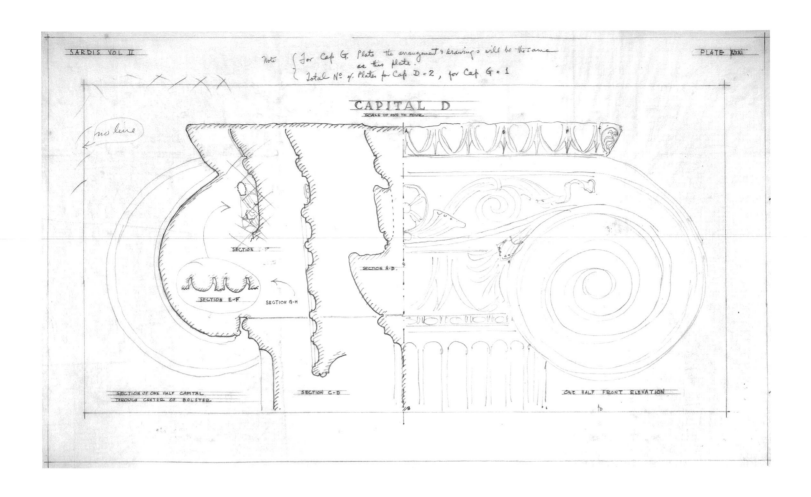

CAPITAL D
SCALE OF ONE TO FOUR

no line

SECTION F

SECTION E-F

SECTION G-H

SECTION A-B

SECTION OF ONE HALF CAPITAL
THROUGH CENTER OF BOLSTER.

SECTION C-D

ONE HALF FRONT ELEVATION

21

TEMPLE OF ARTEMIS: FINISHED DRAW-
ING OF CAPITAL D FOR PLATE XVII IN
BUTLER 1925, ATLAS, 1:2

Gordon McCormick, 1922

Black ink and graphite on thick wove paper

95.1 × 141 cm (37⅛ × 55½ in.)

Department of Art and Archaeology,
Princeton University

This is the finished drawing of capital D, signed by Gordon McCormick, and published (reduced by half to give a scale of 1:4) as plate XVII in the Atlas of Plates. It is based on a number of measured field sketches made in Sardis in 1922 (see cat. 19). Like its preparatory or layout model illustrated in cat. 20, the drawing is a composite showing the right half of the capital in elevation, and several sections taken through the middle of the echinus egg, the center of the volute (with the middle egg seen in elevation), and the middle of the bolster (with the back side and the bottom of the volute in elevation) (see fig. 23). The sections follow exactly the same order as the layout sketch, but they are drawn in hard line to scale and include a detailed rendering of ornament, such as the palmettes and acanthus leaves seen in elevation.

These details, harder to include on measured sketches made in the field or the composite freehand drawing anticipating the final layout of the published plate, were studied and drawn as separate motifs before being incorporated into the final drawing. To study and sketch, sometimes from various angles, an ornamental detail of a large and complex piece—independent of its overall final, composite rendering (an elevation, or a section/elevation)—is quite a common field practice (see cat. 23). These ornamental details, especially the twisted stalks flanking the central rosette, are actually very poorly preserved on capital D; McCormick reconstructed them by comparison with capitals A, C, and E. Capital D is also documented by a quarter reversed plan (bottom) and one-half elevation of its bolster, published as Plate XVIII in the Atlas.   FKY

TEMPLE
OF
ARTEMIS

CAPITAL-D

SCALE 1·4

22

ARCHITECT THROWING STONE OVER COLUMN 7 OF TEMPLE OF ARTEMIS

Lansing C. Holden, 1922

Graphite on wove paper

28.2 × 18 cm (11⅛ × 7⅛ in.)

Anonymous Loan

In the spring of 1922, Lansing "Denny," C. Holden, Jr., and his Princeton roommate Gordon McCormick, both architecture students at the time, made a trip to Sardis in order to "verify several details [of the Temple of Artemis] by further study on the site."[1] No doubt, they were specially selected for this task by H. C. Butler, who had presided over their previous architectural studies at Princeton and who participated in this special trip to Turkey before the publication of the "temple volume" of the Princeton Expedition (Butler died in Paris, in August of the same year, on his way back to the United States, and the Temple was published in 1925). The project was in fact a part of the larger wartime effort of survey, study, and excavation at Sardis, between March and July of 1922, after a seven-year interruption. According to Edward Stoever's field report for 1922, Holden and McCormick "made a much more detailed series of measurements and drawings of the details of the temple."[2] In particular, the two young architects measured and sketched capitals D, E, G, as well as A and B, the latter two preserved in situ on columns 6 and 7. Their field study and sketches became the basis of the finished drawings published in the 1925 Atlas of Plates for *Sardis* vol. 2, *Architecture*, part 1, *The Temple of Artemis* (for the field sketches of capital D, see cat. 19). In a letter written to his mother from Sardis (22 May 1922), Holden described the capitals he had been drawing as "the most beautiful things I have ever seen." Holden's taste in appreciating the extraordinary beauty of classical architecture parallels his teacher's. Another student of Butler, George Howard Forsyth, Jr. (who became a professor of art history at the University of Michigan), recalled Butler as "a mag-

netic teacher and a great stylist," and one of Butler's statements in class as, "Gentlemen, the curve of the echinus of the capitals of the Parthenon is the most beautiful curve in the world."[3]

Of the five capitals drawn on the site by Holden and McCormick, capitals A and B, atop their columns and more than seventeen meters (about fifty-six ft.) above the ground—and probably never reached since the day they were placed there by the Roman work crew—were the most challenging. Capital A (slightly askew on column 6) was "measured" and drawn with the help of photography and transit readings. Capital B was actually reached for direct measurements by Holden, who hoisted himself in a bosun's chair.

The animated sketch by Holden shows him in the act of throwing a stone attached to a string over column 7, which would help to pull the rope and the pulley for the bosun's chair. The four others who watch Holden's energetic attempt must be H. C. Butler, Gordon McCormick, William Berry, and Edward Stoever. It is hard to identify the individuals: who is the person on top of the truncated column (column 8), or the standing figure in front with the handlebar mustache? Which one is Butler? Lansing Holden III, Denny's son, is confident that the seated figure with the cigarette is Gordon McCormick.[4] Between the columns we see the ruins of Church M; high up in the distance, below the faintly sketched towering peak of the Acropolis, is the Expedition house, which had been severely damaged during the continuing Turkish-Greek War and sufficiently repaired in the spring of 1922 for the accommodation of the small party of Expedition members.

To throw a stone over an eighteen-meter-tall column is no easy feat—some of our Expedition members perennially try without even coming close (a slingshot might have been easier, but that is not what the sketch shows). If any one could have achieved it, it would have been Denny Holden, the 26-year-old all-around sportsman, a Princeton flying ace, a much-decorated aviator hero, and a confirmed

risk taker recently out of the Great War. The group's visit to Sardis in April 1922 must have indeed carried certain risks since the Turkish-Greek War was still raging in western Anatolia, and some of the fiercest battles were about to be fought close to Sardis.

In 1992, seventy years after Holden's incredible feat, the Expedition erected a steel pipe scaffolding around columns 6 and 7 in order to provide me far more comfortable and safer access to properly study these capitals. New direct measurements of capital B deviate only slightly from Holden's made under extremely difficult conditions in the bosun's chair. In the crack between the top of column 7 and its capital B, Crawford Greenewalt and I discovered a small zinc plate bearing an inscription in raised letters made by a nail: "L. C. Holden, Jr. / 4.6.1922." The plate was returned to its position out of respect for this brave and talented member of the Butler Expedition who died in a flying accident in 1938.   FKY

1. Butler 1925, Text, vii, Preface by T. L. Shear.
2. Stoever 1922, 7.
3. Personal communication, Crawford H. Greenewalt, Jr.
4. Personal communication, Crawford H. Greenewalt, Jr.

23

TEMPLE OF ARTEMIS: FIELD SKETCHES OF CAPITAL B

Fikret K. Yegül, 1992

Graphite and black ink on Mylar with pressure-sensitive tape

51.6 × 70.3 cm (20⁷/₁₆ × 27⅝ in.)

Archaeological Exploration of Sardis, AT-107B

The recording of complex architectural ornament is often facilitated by a number of separate "parts" sketches in order to help the draftsman to visualize the intricate details when they are committed to hard-line drawings. Not unlike an artist making detail studies of a larger figure on the margins of the sketchpad, making thumbnail sketches in the field is a time-honored tradition in architectural recording and drafting. During their 1922 visit to Sardis, Lansing Holden and Gordon McCormick made many fine parts studies of the Temple capitals, which were later incorporated into final, to-scale sections and elevations and published in the Atlas (see drawings of capital D, almost surely by McCormick, cats. 19–21).

This sheet is a composite of a number of field sketches in pencil made in 1992 depicting the south bolster and southwest volute of capital B on column 7. They were made some seventeen meters (about fifty-six ft.) above the ground, on a scaffold erected to facilitate the study and recording of columns 6 and 7 and their in-situ capitals. Still, certain parts of the intricate ornament, especially the bottoms of the bolsters overhanging the column shaft, were difficult and dangerous to reach in order to make a comprehensive, to-scale drawing. Therefore, I made a dozen or more quick sketches of the parts of capitals A and B, and later incorporated them into full-size, hard-line drawings.

None of these field sketches are drawn to scale, but measurements of their parts are written on them. All are freehand except the upper left one, which is a hard-line elevation of the south bolster, drawn on the scaffold with the help of a ruler, with "eyeballed" proportions, but not to any specific scale. Below this are detail sketches of the egg-and-dart of the abacus, its corner egg, and the double reeds of the bolster. The top center sketch is the southwest corner of the bolster showing the handsome palmettes decorating its curving underside (the same detail used on capital D was sketched by McCormick, see cat. 19A). The center bottom illustration is the corner of the southwest volute and the echinus egg with the leaf ornament at the volute angle (the curling leaf ends are similar to those of capital C, though more pronounced, but unlike those of capital D, where the same leaves have straight, sharp ends and cling tightly to the eggs—this subtle difference was already noted by Butler).[1] The sketch on the upper right is a section through the south volute illustrating the intricate joint between its rounded bottom and the top of the column shaft. The bottom right shows the detail of the "eye" of the southwest volute and a horizontal section through the volute face, giving the dimensions of the spiraling *canalis*, astragal, fillets, and in the center, the eye.

Besides handwritten measurements, many of these details are accompanied by short captions or telegraphic notations written in the field and intended to help at the final drawing stage. All too often though, with the passage of time, a draftsman might find it hard to read and understand his own cryptic messages! Starting their life as simple and temporary drafting aids, some of these sketches retain their charm and immediacy and begin to have a life of their own even after the hard-line drawings based on them have been completed. Some are even published along with the finished formal drawings and become themselves valuable historical records of the process of recording architecture. FKY

1. Butler 1925, Text, 69.

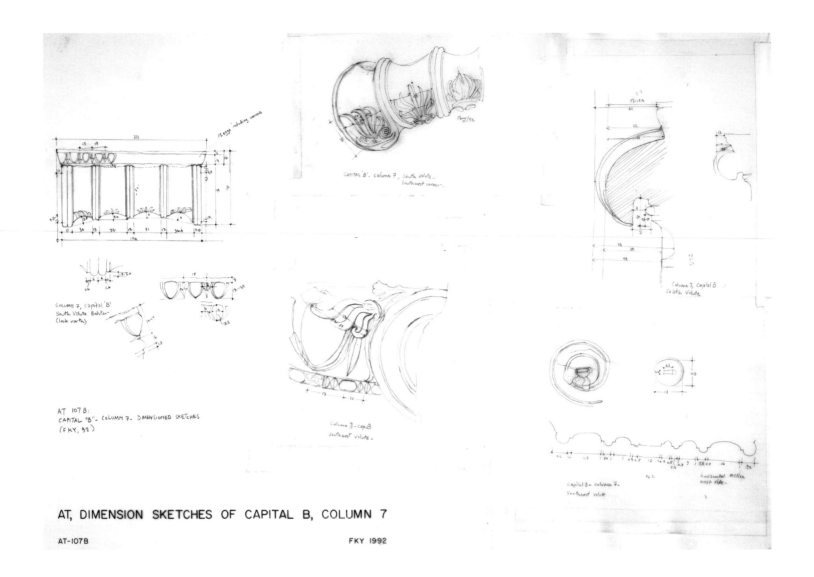

CAPITAL 'B' column 7, South Volute_
Southwest corner_

Column 7, Capital B
South Volute

Column 7, capital 'B'
South Volute Baluster
(look north)

AT 107B:
CAPITAL "B" _ COLUMN 7 _ DIMENSIONED SKETCHES
(FKY, 92)

Column 7 - cap B
Southwest Volute _

Capital B _ column 7 _
Southwest Volute

horizontal section
west side _

AT, DIMENSION SKETCHES OF CAPITAL B, COLUMN 7

AT-107B   FKY 1992

24

Temple of Artemis: Stone-for-stone plan—detail of north half of the crosswall, composite of 16 sheets, 1:20

Fikret K. Yegül, 1996, 1997

Black ink on Mylar

150 × 92 cm (59 × 36¼ in.), sheet;
detail illustrated, 42 × 56 cm (16½ × 22 in.)

Archaeological Exploration of Sardis, AT-96.1–8 A–D3, A–D4; AT-97.1–8 A–D1, A–D2

The plan reproduced here shows the connection of the Temple's north-south crosswall with the long north wall of the cella, and the foundation of interior column 73, located immediately left (west) of the crosswall. Covering an area of about ten by six meters, it represents only a very small portion of the complete plan of the Temple (composed of sixteen sheets, the full 1:20 scale state plan of the temple is 4.88 × 2.23 meters, representing the fourth largest Ionic temple in the world, 97.60 × 44.60 m).

In 1987, the Harvard-Cornell Expedition began a comprehensive project to record graphically and study the Temple of Artemis. The 1:20 scale plan, sections, elevations, and many construction details and perspectives (at 1:20, 1:10, and 1:5 scales), and a set of restoration studies (perspectives, cutaway views, axonometric views) using traditional drafting methods as well as computer-aided layouts based on electronic total station surveying, are among the efforts of our current investigation. It is hoped that such close reading of the building will produce hitherto overlooked information that might illuminate the complex and controversial history of this great building.

Though there were some important preliminary efforts by eighteenth- and nineteenth-century travelers to record the temple (particularly by Giovanni Battista Borra, draftsman on Robert Wood's expedition, and C. R. Cockerell, the eminent English neoclassical architect; see cats. 4, 5), the Temple was excavated, scientifically recorded, and quite sumptuously published by Howard Crosby Butler, the director of the Princeton Expedition.[1] While admirable for the monumental excavation work achieved in a relatively short time and for the detailed stylistic study of the architectural ornament (especially the beautiful Ionic capitals reproduced in the Atlas by large plates), much of the scientific recording of this vast structure was still left undone or incomplete. The best state plan published is 1:200 scale, really not large enough to show any detail in a building of such vast size. The current project is an attempt to remedy this.

The partial plan shown here is the "stone by stone, crack by crack" recording of the top view of the blocks (i.e., not a "horizontal cut" through the building, which is the technical definition of a plan). All visible construction features (clamp holes, dowel holes, lewis holes, mason's marks, tool marks, setting lines, as well as cracks and surface erosion) are faithfully recorded. We can compare our plan with the recording of the same area, with much less detail, by Butler's architects of 1911 recorded in the official Architects' Notebook (see cat. 18).

The area covered in this partial plan—the junction of the crosswall that divides the cella into two exactly equal parts, and the long north wall of the cella—is of critical importance in elucidating the building history based on the peculiarities and details of construction. For instance, the north end of the crosswall does not bond into the north wall except where a ten-centimeter-wide notch cut on the north wall side "receives" the end block(s) of the crosswall above the foundation course, indicating that these two walls are not contemporaneous. Both have been preserved at the top foundation course, one course below the level of the finished paving of the cella. However, the blocks of the missing bottom course are attested by their clear impressions on the top surface of the crosswall. There is also a noticeable difference in construction features and style between the two walls: the main north wall is composed of much larger blocks fitted closely (especially true for the lower course shown along the top end of the wall); no lewis holes for lifting have been used. The top course blocks are joined by simple I-clamps arranged in a row along their southern (inner) side. The blocks of the 0.90-meter-wide crosswall are much smaller; every block has a lewis hole, and they are secured to each other by at least one, but often by two, three, or even four, large butterfly-type clamps. The north wall displays a systematic use of small, square dowel holes in combination with leverage slits (each dowel hole/leverage slit combination signifies the position of the edge of the block above it). There are leverage slits but no dowel holes in the crosswall. The foundation for the interior column 73, pushed against the foundations of the crosswall, is similar in construction features and style to the north wall and indicates contemporaneity of the north wall of the cella and the interior columns. Construction evidence elsewhere in the Temple, as well as on the site and in the larger regional context of western Asia Minor, suggests that the main walls of the cella and the interior columns (though preserved only in their foundations) belong to the original Hellenistic construction; the crosswall came later as part of a major reorganization and reconstruction of the temple during the Roman imperial period.
FKY

1. Butler 1922; Butler 1925.

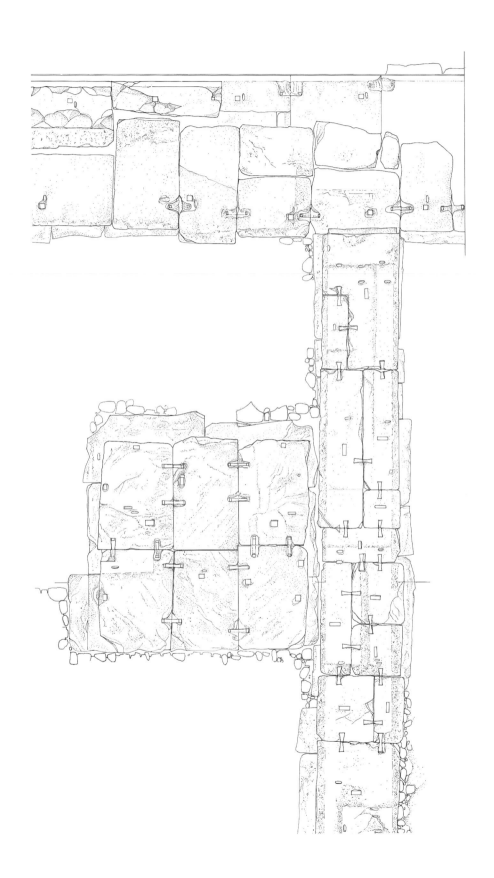

25

Temple of Artemis: South wall
exterior elevation—detail of
southeast anta and column number 17, composite, four sections,
1:20

Fikret K. Yegül, 1998

Black ink on Mylar

92 × 160 cm (36¼ × 63 in.), sheet;
detail illustrated: 43 × 56 cm (17 × 22 in.)

Archaeological Exploration of Sardis,
AT-98.7–10 D1–4

Illustrating the east end of the south wall,
the southeast anta pier, and column 17,
this detail shows a small portion of the
long south elevation of the Temple (the full
elevation drawing is 4.88 m at 1:20 scale;
shown in this exhibition reduced to 60
percent it is 2.93 m; see fig. 17). Reaching
a height of about 4.88 meters in six or
seven courses, this is the best preserved,
and one of the most beautiful and representative examples of Greek marble masonry in the Aegean—the wall that Cyriacus of Ancona, who visited the site in
1444, had described as "extraordinarily
elegant."[1]

The long south wall of the cella rests on
a slightly projecting stylobate (effectively,
the line is approx. five to eight cm above
the ground line in the drawing). It has a
high base molding in two courses (1.10 m
high) and is crowned by a handsome, but
partially finished, rounded profile known
as a torus. Above the torus line are two
courses of massive marble blocks (0.88 m
and 0.76 m high) with smoothly finished
surfaces and almost imperceptible joints
achieved by the ingenious Greek masonry
technique called *anathyrosis* (an exception-
ally smooth dressing of only the margins
of the blocks, the middle parts are recessed
and do not touch each other) visible only
where the ends of the blocks are exposed.
The bottom of the lower course, above the
torus, has a fillet and a smooth outward
and upward curve called an *apophyge*.
These two courses can be conceived as a
kind of *orthostate* or dado. Above this, the
fifth, sixth, and seventh courses have been
treated in a more decorative fashion: marble blocks are "drafted" or trimmed with
thin, smooth bands (approx. 8–10 cm)
that surround and define slightly raised
rectangular panels in the middle. This
well-known Greek ashlar masonry technique articulates the wall surface by crisp
lines of light and shadow and creates an il-
lusion of mass—in Butler's admiring words
it "serves to accentuate strongly the structure of the walls."[2] The terminating anta
pier, projecting a mere four to five centimeters beyond the wall surface, con-
trasted the textured expanse of the wall by
its exceptional smooth finish.

Column 17, preserved at a height of
6.72 meters (in five drums over a base
1.10 m high), is in line with the east exten-
sion of the anta pier, and in line with
columns 13 and 6, not shown in this detail. Like many of the other columns of the
Temple's east end, column 17 is partially
finished: its shaft remains unfluted; the
double scotias of its Ionic-Asiatic base are
blocked out but not fully shaped and pol-
ished; the lifting bosses of the base (lumps
projecting just below the torus; two of the
usual four are in view) are left in place;
likewise, the rough, projecting band above
the plinth has not been chiseled down and
smoothed. The thin, rectangular "box"
in the upper middle of the plinth represents an ancient repair. The inscription
"MECKEAC" carved on the rough area
of the plinth is understood by Butler's epi-
graphists as "μὲ σκιᾶς" or "Mayst thou
shade me," a comment addressed by the
plinth to the column or portico of the temple.[3] The torus terminating the base is decorated with "water-leaves" with rounded
ends; the same decoration is used on the
torus of column 16, the pendant of our
column in front of the northeast anta pier
(out of the fifteen bases preserved in the
east end of the Temple, the torus decorations of nine have been finished in different stages; six have been left plain). The
smooth band encircling the bottom of the
column shaft at thirty-eight centimeters
above the base and marked by extremely
fine horizontal and vertical lines (not
shown in the drawing) represents the
intended bottom diameter, or the girth, of
the column, and evidently provides guide-
lines for the masons for laying out the
fillets and flutes.

Three vertically stacked grooves visible
on the left side of the shaft, between the
second, third, and fourth joints, represent
an ingenious construction detail to help
the exact placement of the heavy drums on
top of one another. Carved on opposite
sides of a drum, these grooves consist of a
four-to-five-centimeter-long slit on the top
edge of the lower drum and a matching
vertical cut, about ten to fifteen centimeters high, on the drum above. A pair of
crowbars "anchored" at these leverage
slits, pushing against the sloping surface of
the vertical grooves, could guide the partially suspended upper drum into place
and complete the hair-fine adjustment of
the joint once the heavy block was low-
ered. The crude square hole in the middle
of the fourth drum was probably a notch
for a wooden beam of a temporary, later
structure, built long after the Temple was
abandoned and possibly partially destroyed. Similar, matching square beam
holes have been found on many of the east
end columns.   FKY

1. Cyriac of Ancona forthcoming.
2. Butler 1925, Text, 32.
3. Buckler and Robinson 1932, 144–45, no. 182, with
   the column misidentified as number 16.

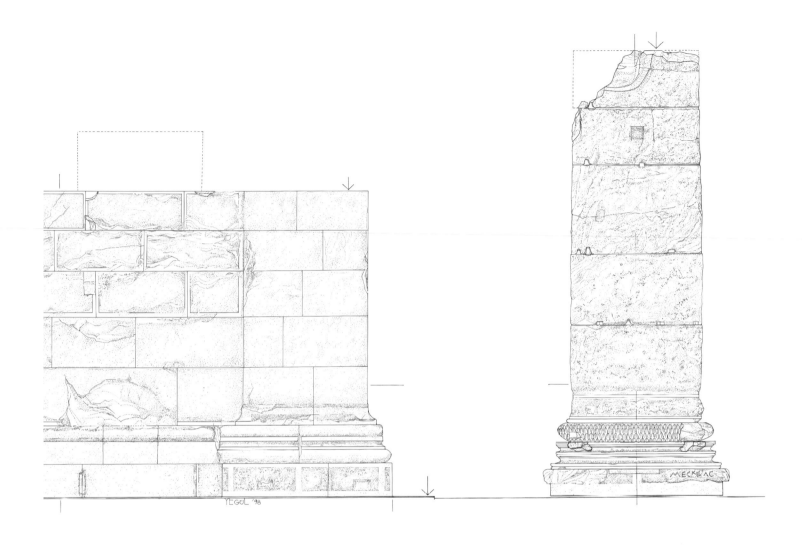

YEGÜL '98

MECKE AC

26

Temple of Artemis: East elevation
of columns 8, 7, and 6, 1:20

Fikret K. Yegül, 1999

Black ink on Mylar

120.1 × 88 cm (47¼ × 34⅝ in.)

Archaeological Exploration of Sardis, A1-99.1

"The twin columns which, rising out of a sloping field beside the Paktolos, have long marked the site of the more ancient city of Sardis, are of the Ionic order with unfluted, and consequently unfinished, shafts," wrote Butler in 1910, before the excavation started, describing the general state of archaeological remains in Sardis.[1] These are indeed the two columns privileged by their near perfect state of preservation, and featured in many of the early travelers' drawings, most prominently in the drawings of G. B. Borra (1750) and C. R. Cockerell (1812), and most dramatically in the 1835 watercolor by C. F. Stanfield (cats. 4, 5; fig. 11). Such was the influence of these powerful columns on all who had seen, depicted, and wished to excavate them that at the end of the second season of excavations, Butler jubilantly announced that the base of one of the standing columns (number 7) was revealed "for the first time," and noted the exact date, 17 June 1911.[2] The following year both columns 6 and 7 were fully excavated. In an earlier effort to explore the Temple on behalf of the Imperial Ottoman Museums, Gustave Mendel, in 1904, had opened a deep pit against the north flank of column 6 and had already exposed its base.[3]

The finished ink drawing of the elevation, completed in 1999, shows three of the southernmost columns of the east peristyle looking to the west: the left, truncated column is number 8; the middle is column 7; the right, its capital shifted southward, is column 6. The latter two columns and their capitals became the subjects of a special study in 1992–93 when a pipe scaffold was erected around them in order to allow their full and detailed measurements to be taken and drawings made (cat. 23). In 1922, however, capital B on

column 7 had been reached using a bosun's chair by Lansing C. Holden, Jr., although the difficult conditions of the exercise limited the amount of recording that could be done (see cat. 22).

The total height of the intact columns (with bases and capitals) is 17.81 meters, almost exactly sixty Roman feet. Their diameters taper from 2.005 meters at the bottom to 1.76 meters at the top with a distinct possibility of the use of entasis (diameters of drums 4–5 m above ground are slightly larger than bottom diameters, even in their roughly shaped, unfinished state). The columns of the Temple of Artemis in Sardis are among the tallest and most monumental of ancient columns (the Athenian Parthenon's Doric columns are 10.35 m tall; the Artemision in Ephesos had Ionic columns of 17.52 m; the Corinthian columns of Zeus Olympios in Athens are 16.75 m; only the Ionic columns of the Temple of Apollo at Didyma at 19.55 m are significantly taller than those of the Sardian Artemis). The shifted capital A of column 6 (the one described by Richard Chandler, who had visited the site in 1764, as "one with the capital awry to the south,"[4]) is carved in one piece with the top drum of the shaft, the only such capital detail we know from the Temple. The fluting below the capitals of both columns conform to a well-utilized construction principle in classical architecture: on the topmost drum of the shaft a master mason lays out and starts the flutes and the fillets (usually twenty-four in number), which are subsequently carved in situ. The top drum of column 7 displays numerous very fine vertical lines, marking the axes of the column as well as the widths of flutes and fillets, that probably were to guide the masons (strings might have been stretched down from these neck markings to indicate the gradual widening of fluting).

As in all other 1:20 scale drawings of the Temple, these column elevations attempt to record surface tooling of the unfinished drums, construction and setting lines, later cuts, abrasions, and cracks, as well as occasional graffiti carved on their

surfaces. Vertical grooves paired with leverage slits carved between the joints of drums were used for the delicate operation of levering and moving the heavy drums in order to make fine adjustments in their positions. The top (plan) view of column 8 (left) shows the circular *anathyrosis* of the drum at their horizontal joints (the middle, roughly finished circle is recessed); a large lewis hole in the center was for lifting; two smaller, square dowel holes on opposite sides of the center secured the drums against lateral movement. All three bases, of the Ionic-Asiatic type, have the same height (1.12 m), but only the torus of column 6 has been finished with decorative oak leaves.   FKY

1. Butler 1922, 25.
2. Butler 1922, 72, fig. 68.
3. Mendel 1905.
4. Quoted in Butler 1922, 25.

Fig. 24. View of the Synagogue and Marble Court after restoration (1973).

Dashed Lines

Crawford H. Greenewalt, Jr.

"Dashed Lines" is the cipher for interpretive drawings and reconstructions, derived from the convention of using a dashed or broken line to show hypothetical, unconfirmed forms. All ancient buildings at Sardis, like most at other sites, are very incomplete. Their lowest parts often survive but rarely stand much more than a meter (about three feet) above ancient ground level. Sometimes, by no means always, fallen parts provide evidence for the form, materials, and size of what no longer stands. Some fallen parts survive in intact assemblages—like a large segment of the brick-and-mortar north wall of the Synagogue (cats. 39–41), which provided evidence for the height of that wall—others in isolated, scattered elements, the relationship of which can be established from design, decoration, and construction features (the last notably in corresponding clamp and dowel holes)—like the column and entablature blocks of the Marble Court in the Roman Bath-Gymnasium Complex (cats. 35–38).

Reconstruction drawings can show helpfully and vividly how ruined buildings once looked; they can be equally instructive in clarifying how such buildings could not have looked, and in revealing the biases of archaeologists and the limitations of information available to the artist.

The aim of the drawing and the amount of evidence preserved govern the degree of resolution in reconstructions. Hans Buchwald's reconstruction of the thirteenth-century Byzantine church, Church E, partly based on fallen wall, vault, and dome fragments and on closely similar churches at other sites, reveals its richness of form and decoration, which only a specialist art historian could guess from its standing lower walls and fallen, fragmentary upper parts (cat. 42; fig. 29). Fikret K. Yegül's reconstructions of the ceremonial hall, the Marble Court, in the Roman Bath-Gymnasium Complex (cats. 36, 37) were made in anticipation of full-scale physical reconstruction. Monte Antrim's reconstruction of the Lydian city wall (cat. 30) particularly aimed to show wooden shutters in the battlements, for which evidence had recently been uncovered (see Catherine Alexander's drawing, cat. 31), and, for the sake of consistency, other features were rendered with the same specificity. James Anderson's reconstruction of the Synagogue interior (cat. 40) was made to show particular architectural features and ornament that survived in scattered fragments and that provide evidence for a lofty, lavishly decorated interior. Conversely, in Philip Stinson's reconstructions of the Lydian city wall (cat. 29) and Elizabeth

Fig. 25. Marble Court, photomontage showing architectural fragments (1961).

Fig. 26. Marble Court, exposed architectural fragments of the Marble Court in situ (1961).

Wahle's reconstruction of Lydian installations for refining precious metals (cat. 27), sketchy or cartoonlike drawing styles emphasize limitations of evidence.

Two-dimensional reconstructions in sketches and drawings often are sufficient to combine evidence of different kinds and to explain ideas, and they are relatively inexpensive and easy to store. The validity of reconstructions can be more thoroughly tested with three-dimensional scale models, like that of the Synagogue (cat. 39), even more so with full-scale reconstructions (like those of the Synagogue and the Marble Court of the Bath-Gymnasium Complex; figs. 24, 27, 28). Full-scale reconstructions comprehensively address issues of structure and enforce confrontation with details, which in two-dimensional drawings with a single viewpoint can be concealed or ignored. Reconstruction of the Marble Court required thorough understanding of its magnificent columnar and aedicular facade, which survived as a disorderly tumble of fallen marble blocks (figs. 25, 26); following excavation, the first step in reconstruction was a graphic recording of all blocks (cat. 35). The arcuated pediment at first was incorrectly associated with the first story (cats. 36, 37); its correct association with the second story (cat. 38; fig. 27), became clear only through the physical reassembly of the blocks.

27

SECTOR PN: LYDIAN INDUSTRIAL AREA, REFINING PRECIOUS METALS AT SARDIS IN THE AGE OF CROESUS

Elizabeth G. Wahle, 1975; Catherine S. Alexander, 1998

Black ink with traces of graphite and white correction fluid on white wove paper

44.2 × 58.6 cm (17¼ × 23¼ in.)

Archaeological Exploration of Sardis, PN-111

Published in Hanfmann 1983, fig. 139; Ramage and Ramage 1983, fig. 5; Ramage and Craddock 2000, fig. 10.1.

Excavation during the 1960s and 1970s (mainly 1968 and 1969) in a region of the city site located near the east bank of the Pactolus Stream, outside the Lydian city wall, uncovered remains of construction and artifacts datable to the first half of the sixth century B.C. and associated with the refining of gold and silver. The remains included at least nine mudbrick furnaces in two clusters, more than a hundred small, basin-shaped and clay-lined hollows in the ancient occupation surface, blowpipe and bellows nozzles, vitrified ceramic items, lead litharge, and more than three hundred small pieces of gold in the form of globules, driblets, and foil. Even before the gold appeared in quantity, excavator Andrew Ramage speculated that the material might be associated with working gold; conservator Richard Stone suggested that the basinlike hollows might be cupels, used in a metallurgical separating process called cupellation. Further research confirmed and elaborated on those identifications.

The remains evidently had been used in the separation—or parting—of gold and silver from alluvial gold, which contains a certain proportion of silver. As reconstructed by Paul Craddock (British Museum Laboratories) and Ramage, gold and silver were parted in the furnaces through a process called cementation: foils of alluvial gold were sandwiched between layers of salt and subjected to a low heat for several days, as a result of which the silver was converted to silver chloride and the gold was left in a relatively pure state. To recover metallic silver from the silver chloride, the latter was smelted with lead, thereby producing a mixture of metallic silver and lead; the mixture then was cupelled—placed in the basinlike cupels and subjected to intense heat and oxygen, by means of bellows and blowpipes—thereby parting the silver and lead. Cupellation might also have been used before the cementation process, to part base metal (copper) present in the alluvial gold. These remains provide the earliest known evidence for the cementation process. Ramage and Craddock suggest that the process was developed in response to a perceived need for metallic purity in coinage and led to the beginning of bimetallic currency in gold and silver. Subsequently, Craddock has suggested that alluvial gold was also being refined by the Lydians to make coins of electrum, the artificial alloy of gold and silver.[1]

The reconstruction drawing shows, at far left, alluvial gold being hammered into foil in preparation for cementation; at center, cupellation; and, in the background, the cementation furnaces. At far right is an altar, ornamented with small limestone statues of lions; most of the altar and parts of the lions survive. The altar probably was associated with the goddess Kuvava/Cybele. It is marginally later in date than the metallurgical activity; excavator Ramage has speculated that it might have been built as an offering of thanks for success in the cementation process. The drawing conveys the informality of the setting in which the gold refining activity seems to have occurred: there is no obvious organization to furnace assemblages and cupellation zones, and no evidence for boundary walls that might define and control the activity.

The drawing is one of three made in 1975 by Elizabeth Wahle, in consultation with Ramage (for the architectural setting) and conservator Sidney M. Goldstein (for technical features); later, after it was realized that one-handled cooking pots had commonly been used in the cementation process, handles were added to representations of those (four) pots. The other two drawings show a more general view and a detail of the cementation process.[2] CHG

1. See Craddock, Cowell, and Guerra forthcoming.
2. Published in Greenewalt 1977, figs. 10, 11.

28

Tumulus at Bin Tepe, locally
called Karniyarik Tepe: Imaginary
view with separated upper and
lower parts

Crawford H. Greenewalt, Jr., 1965

Black ink with traces of graphite on wove paper

35 × 50 cm (13¾ × 19¾ in.)

Archaeological Exploration of Sardis, BT-62

Published in Hanfmann 1972, fig. 108.

With a base diameter of approximately 220 meters (about 720 ft.) and a height of approximately 50 meters (about 165 ft.), Karnıyarık Tepe ("split-belly mound," so called from deep gashes in its sides) is one of three extra-large tumuli in the Bin Tepe tumulus cemetery. In hopes that its large size had frustrated tomb robbers' attempts to locate and loot the burial chamber (as has been the case with most of the smaller tumuli), and that modern methods might succeed where ancient ones had failed, the Sardis Expedition explored the tumulus during several seasons: geophysical survey in 1963; excavation, by tunneling, in 1964–66; ground-penetrating radar survey, inside the Expedition tunnels, in 1992; and drilling/coring, to identify anomalies detected in the radar survey, in 1995. None of those attempts succeeded in locating the burial chamber. Excavation did reveal, however, an unfinished circular retaining wall (crepis), concentric within the circle of the mound exterior (the long curved section of tunnel runs along the outer face of the retaining wall), which evidently had been built to curb an earlier, smaller version of the tumulus, and a system of ancient tunnels that had been dug—by grave robbers, or ancient excavators?—in Roman times. (A Roman water jug was recovered intact and upright, in a niche that had been hollowed in the side of one of the ancient tunnels.)

Unlike other interpretive drawings in the exhibition, this sketch was made for Expedition workmen, to clarify the location within the mound of the tunnels that they were digging. For two excavation seasons, it was posted next to a measured plan of the tunnels, at the main tunnel entrance. It shows the upper part of the tumulus as if sliced through and raised. Several of the figures represent specific individuals. The man chopping wood, to make the log posts that shored up the tunnel at two-meter intervals, is Eyup Gürleyen, a miner from the lignite mines at Soma, northeast of Sardis, who had been hired by the Expedition to supervise tunnel digging. The seated figure, gesticulating to a group in the foreground, was a spellbinding chatterbox who distracted others. Outside a kitchen building, the cook prepares dinner. Taking the air on the mound summit is the Turkish commissioner (government representative) for excavation in Karnıyarık Tepe, Muharrem Tağtekin (curator in the Archaeological and Ethnographical Museum in Manisa).

The small figure at upper left represents King Gyges of Lydia (reigned c. 687–652 B.C.), who, at the time the drawing was made, was thought to have been buried in the mound (a mason's mark that recurs several times on the crepis wall—and that appears twice under Gyges's figure here—was read by Expedition members as a monogram for "Gugu," Gyges's name in Akkadian). His anachronistic hookah or narghile was a conceit of miner Eyup ("we'll find Gyges smoking his narghile") and prompted the Arabian Nights dress. The mound was probably created a century after Gyges's time, perhaps for a prince in the last generation of the Mermnad dynasty (Croesus's unfortunate son Atys, who would have died c. 550 B.C., or soon thereafter?).[1]

The labels read as follows: "If the tumulus is thought of as sliced through at the tunnel ceilings, a bird's-eye view of the tumulus would look like this" (upper left) and "This bird is flying north" (lower right).   CHG

1. Ratté 1994.

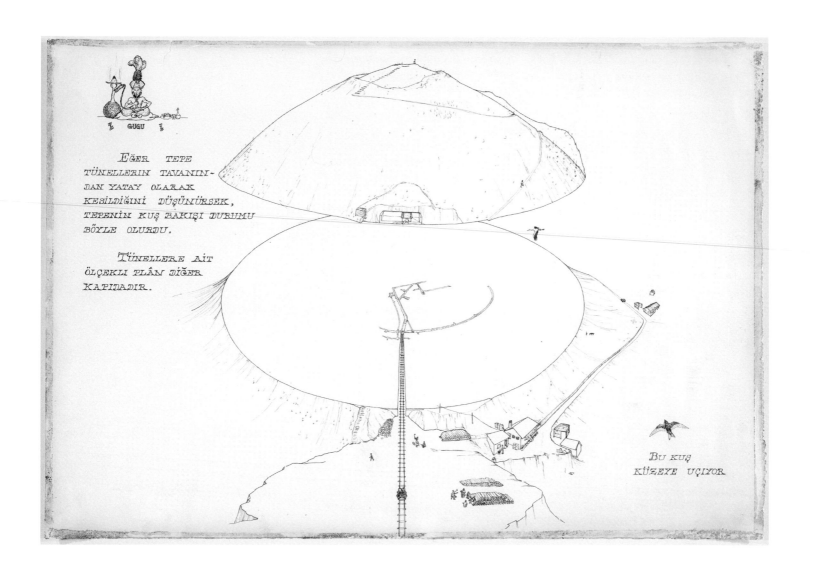

EĞER TEPE
TÜNELLERIN TAVANIN-
DAN YATAY OLARAK
KESILDIĞINI DÜŞÜNÜRSEK,
TEPENIN KUŞ BAKIŞI DURUMU
BÖYLE OLURDU.

TÜNELLERE AIT
ÖLÇEKLI PLÂN DIĞER
KAPIDADIR.

BU KUŞ
KÜZEYE UÇIYOR

29A

Sectors MMS and MMS/N:
Impressionistic reconstruction
of Sardis city defenses before
destruction in the mid-sixth
century b.c., view to east

Philip T. Stinson, 1997

Black ink faded to purple on yellow wove paper

30.4 × 47 cm (12 × 18¼ in.)

Archaeological Exploration of Sardis, MMS/N-42A

29B

Sectors MMS and MMS/N:
Impressionistic reconstruction
of Sardis city defenses before
destruction in the mid-sixth
century b.c., view to west

Philip T. Stinson, 1997

Black ink faded to purple on yellow wove paper

30.5 × 40.6 cm (11⅞ × 16 in.)

Archaeological Exploration of Sardis, MMS/N-42B

Published in Greenewalt 2000, fig. 6a and b.

These reconstructed perspective views of
Lydian city defenses, i.e., wall and earthwork glacis, focus on a segment that contained a gate on the west side of the city
(Sector MMS/N, see Introduction), which,
at that time, was where most of the evidence for the defenses had been uncovered. Construction was massive near the
gate; evidence recovered after these views
had been made indicates that the wall,
twenty meters (sixty-five ft.) thick, originally stood to a height of more than fifteen
meters (fifty ft.), perhaps closer to thirty
meters (ninety-nine ft.). On the high
ground of lower Acropolis slopes (not
shown in these views), the wall was sometimes—not always—considerably less
thick. In 29A the view was designed to illustrate the idea that the wall continued to
the east (not to the west, as in an earlier
reconstruction, cat. 30).

The sketchy quality of the drawings is
meant to communicate limited understanding of some design aspects. Fading
lines of receding defenses in 29A, for example, are consistent with slight evidence
for the defenses on the northeast side of
the site.

Although drawn in about forty-five
minutes, both views were generated from a
three-dimensional computer model, the
underlying computer study for which had
been prepared during several seasons of
collaboration between Expedition architects and excavators. The perspective of
the views is partly based on electronic surveying (at times conducted with transit
and architect precariously poised on
wooden scaffolding above excavation
trenches five meters [about fifteen ft.]
deep).   CHG, PTS

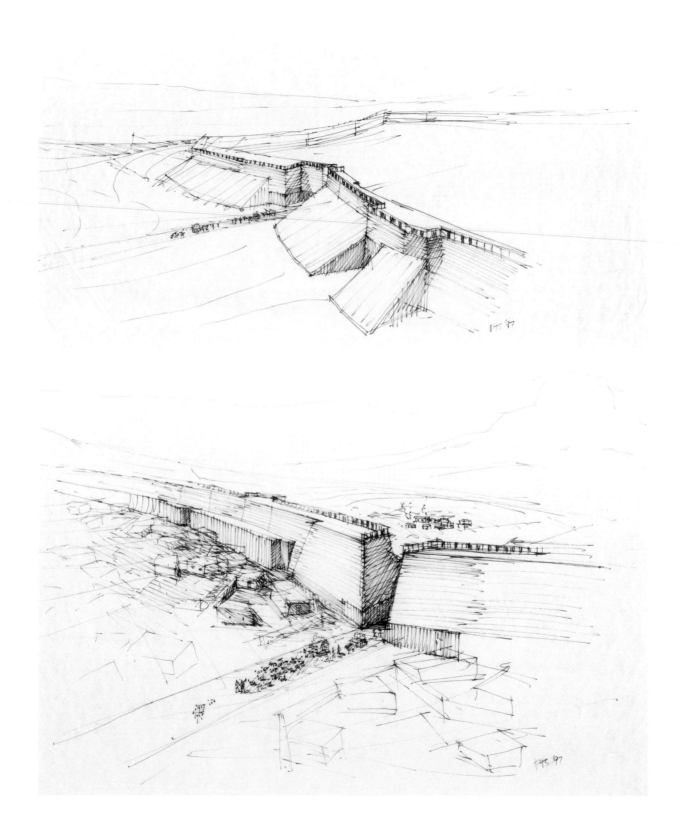

30

SECTORS MMS AND MMS/N: LYDIAN
CITY DEFENSES (WALL AND EARTH-
WORK GLACIS), C. 550 B.C., RECON-
STRUCTED VIEW LOOKING NORTH

Monte D. Antrim, 1990

Black ink on Mylar

68.3 × 60.5 cm (26⅝ × 23⅝ in.)

Archaeological Exploration of Sardis, MMS-70

Published in Greenewalt 1991, fig. 7.

This reconstruction shows city defenses on
the west side of the site (MMS and
MMS/N) and illustrates two misconcep-
tions, which evidence from later excavation has dispelled. In 1990, the year of this
drawing, the core of urban Sardis was
commonly thought to lie west of the defenses, and for that reason the defense line
turns left at the top of the drawing. An
earthwork with sloping surface was
thought to have existed on each side of the
wall: a reinforcing *agger* on the inside, a
defensive glacis on the outside. Subsequent
excavation showed that an earthwork existed only on the west side (i.e., to the left
in this reconstruction).

The drawing also shows wood and
iron-nail assemblages—of which remnants
had been recovered in excavation on the
occupation surface of the "recess" (cat.
31)—as shutters in the battlement embrasures and a door in a (hypothetical)
building behind the battlements. The Expedition Land Rover, following the Lydian
procession on the road, was included
partly for fun, partly to remind viewers
that the image is an interpretation.   CHG

COLOSSAL LYDIAN STRUCTURE
INTERPRETIVE RECONSTRUCTION LOOKING NORTH

MDA 1990

SECTOR MMS: RECONSTRUCTED
WOODEN SHUTTERS AND DOOR FROM
LYDIAN FORTIFICATION WALL—RECESS
IN WALL, PRESERVED NAIL AND RECON-
STRUCTED SHUTTER, RECESS WITH
NAILS AS FOUND, 1:2 AND 1:20

Catherine S. Alexander, 2003

Black ink on Mylar

75.3 × 56.6 cm (29⅝ × 22¼ in.)

Archaeological Exploration of Sardis, MMS-148

The three drawings on this sheet show the
findspots of iron nails discovered in a recess in the western, exterior side of the
Lydian city defenses (wall and earthwork
glacis) and reconstructions of the shutters
and door to which they may have belonged. When excavated, the recess was
filled with destruction debris, consisting
mostly of mudbrick that had formed the
upper part of the fortification wall and
had been demolished and dumped when
the defenses were partly destroyed in the
middle of the sixth century B.C., probably
when the Persians attacked and captured
Sardis in the 540s B.C. Dumped destruction debris of the same kind, on the other
side of the defenses, is shown in cat. 16.
Resting on the occupation surface underneath the debris were many iron nails in
discrete rows or grids of approximately
shutter or door size, with woody remains
around and between the nails. The nails
rested in vertical positions, in each assemblage either pointed-end up or pointed-end
down. These nails and woody remains
may have belonged to shutters that closed
battlement embrasures at the top of the
wall and to a door to a hypothetical building behind the battlements (as reconstructed in cat. 30) and that fell on the
surface of the recess when the defenses
were partly destroyed.   CHG

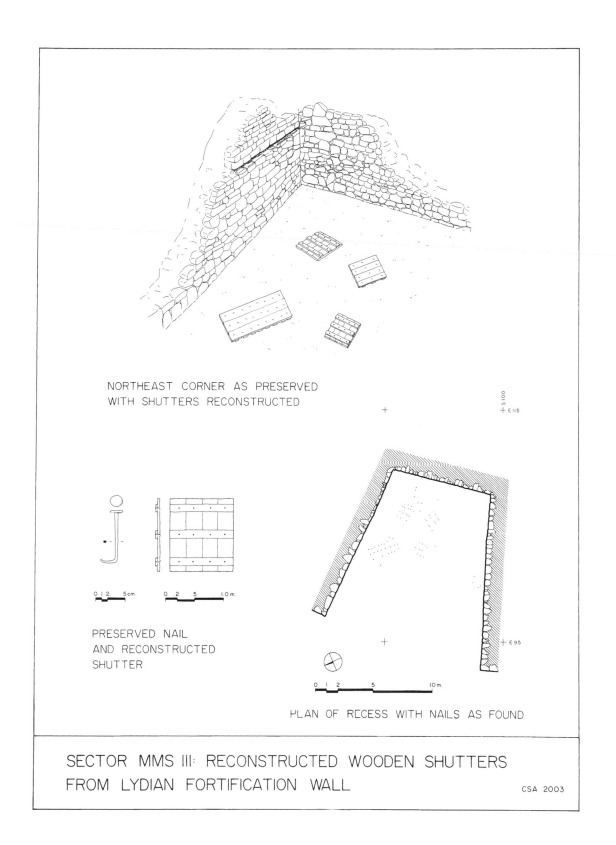

NORTHEAST CORNER AS PRESERVED
WITH SHUTTERS RECONSTRUCTED

+ S 100
+ E 115

+

0 1 2 5cm.   0 2 5   1.0 m.

PRESERVED NAIL
AND RECONSTRUCTED
SHUTTER

+

⊕

0 1 2   5   10 m.

+ E 95

PLAN OF RECESS WITH NAILS AS FOUND

SECTOR MMS III: RECONSTRUCTED WOODEN SHUTTERS
FROM LYDIAN FORTIFICATION WALL

CSA 2003

32

SECTOR MMS/N: GATEWAY IN THE LY-
DIAN CITY WALL, SEEN FROM OUTSIDE,
MID-SIXTH CENTURY B.C., INTERPRE-
TIVE RECONSTRUCTION LOOKING EAST

Philip T. Stinson, 1992

Black ink with traces of graphite on yellow wove paper

18.5 × 22.1 cm (7¼ × 8¾ in.)

Archaeological Exploration of Sardis, MMS/N-24

Published in Greenewalt 1993, fig. 4.

This reconstruction was made together
with that in cat. 33 to suggest the appearance of the gateway in city defenses on the
west side of the site (MMS, companion
sector MMS/N) before and immediately
after destruction in the mid-sixth century
B.C. Here the gateway is depicted before
destruction, in about 550 B.C. The wall,
reconstructed at fourteen meters (about
forty-six ft.), should be higher (see cat.
29). The system for closing the gate has
not been determined. Doors or a portcullis
may have existed in the gate passage, but
no trace of them has as yet been identified.
(The docile, yaklike draft animal, hauling
stone for use in the construction of the
glacis at right, is a pleasant conceit of
architect Stinson.)   CHG, PTS

33

SECTOR MMS/N: GATE LOCATION IN THE LYDIAN CITY WALL BEING BLOCKED AFTER DESTRUCTION, MID-SIXTH CENTURY B.C., INTERPRETIVE RECONSTRUCTION LOOKING EAST

Philip T. Stinson, 1992

Black ink with traces of graphite on yellow wove paper

18.6 × 22.1 cm (7¼ × 8¾ in.)

Archaeological Exploration of Sardis, MMS/N-24A

Published in Greenewalt 1993, fig. 4.

This reconstruction shows the same location and view as in cat. 32. Here the gateway in the Lydian city wall is being eliminated by blockage, in the form of a massive casemate construction (a pair of walls 3.30 meters [ten ft.] thick framing a core of loose stone fill) in the gate court (cf. cat. 11). The relationship of the blockage to the major destruction of the Lydian defenses in the mid-sixth century B.C. was uncertain during several years of excavation. Had the gate been blocked by the Sardians in anticipation of attack and siege, or after destruction, when city defenses were rebuilt? The distinctive destruction debris of tumbled, semibaked mudbrick at first had seemed to be pressed against the outside of the stone blockage, as if it postdated the blockage construction, but the presence of a thin layer of destruction debris underneath blockage construction indicates that the blockage is post-destruction and had been sunk into the debris. The destruction may be identified with the siege and capture of Sardis by the Persians in the 540s B.C. CHG, PTS

34

Sector MMS/N: Late Roman
Avenue or Plaza, Interpretive
Reconstruction Looking East

Philip T. Stinson, 1993

Black ink with traces of graphite on yellow wove paper

28.5 × 21.9 cm (11¼ × 8⁹/₁₆ in.)

Archaeological Exploration of Sardis, MMS/N-24B

This reconstruction shows the same location and direction of view as in cats. 32 and 33. It was made to show the appearance of the location a thousand years later, in the fifth century A.D. A Roman avenue or plaza and portico now occupy the site. They were built—largely of spoils from older Roman buildings—over the truncated stump of the Lydian gate and its blockage. The repair of Roman water pipes beneath the plaza paving, in progress at left, reveals remnants of the blockage; this scenario was staged by the draftsman in order to visually link this reconstruction with the two previous drawings.   CHG, PTS

MARBLE COURT: REGISTER BOOK OF
ARCHITECTURAL FRAGMENTS, P. 30

Stephen W. Jacobs, 1961–63

Bound volume, graphite on ruled wove paper

34 × 26 cm (13¼ × 10¼ in), page

Archaeological Exploration of Sardis

"Virtually every visitor has hailed this Gymnasium Complex as one of the greatest monuments of Roman Imperial architectural design. It will be a goal of future campaigns to complete excavation of its major features. Then for the reconstruction—for which Steve Jacobs is now laying research foundations." The "Register Book of Architectural Fragments" of which this is a page represents the first steps of solid research about which George M. A. Hanfmann wrote with such panache in 1961.[1] By 1960 the excavations in the Roman Bath-Gymnasium Complex, which had started in 1958, had laid bare the area named the Marble Court, facing the great palaestra of the complex. Some one thousand or so fallen pieces of marble architectural ornament filled the vast space wall to wall, "toppled and twisted in wild mountains of marble," creating an impressive and daunting scene (figs. 25, 26).[2] As it quickly became apparent to A. Henry Detweiler—the Expedition's associate director and an architect with a long field experience in the Roman East, where this sort of columnar, "baroque" architecture was popular during the imperial period—the Marble Court was a spectacular example of multistory columnar facade architecture (sometimes described as "Asiatic marble facades") from the Severan period. The restoration of this high, walled enclosure with elaborate two-story facades of alternating aediculae—encouraged, even demanded, by the Turkish Ministry of Culture—was conceived in three stages: a) the recording and cataloguing of the architectural elements from the Marble Court; b) the determination of the original design based on the study of the remains; c) the actual reconstruction in the field.

This thick sketchbook, or register/catalogue, in which some eight hundred pieces were entered, represents the first stage of this program. It was prepared between 1961 and 1963 by Stephen Jacobs, a professor of architecture at Cornell University and a colleague of Detweiler. Recorded in a standard accountant's ledger, the modest format belies the monumental undertaking it represents and its critical importance for all subsequent aspects of the Marble Court project, study, design, and construction. In the register, each block was assigned a serial number and identified with an abbreviated letter/number code and described in a few words; the findspot was recorded according to the north-south/east-west grid system established for the site. Furthermore, in order to facilitate the location of each block in relation to the room's architecture, the Marble Court (a rectangular space 35.80 × 18.40 m) was divided into eight numbered zones, such as S-NE, S-SE, or N-NE, N-SE, etc. (the southern group of four quadrants is located south of the east-west central axis of the court, numbers one through four; the northern group is on the north, numbers five through eight). Each block was sketched freehand (generally a three-quarter "typical" view exposing maximum ornament, and a separate section-elevation view), and measurements were included on the drawing. Next, each block was moved out of the Court and laid out in the palaestra according to architectural type (represented by its alphabetical letter and number code: A–F were reserved for base elements; G–L for vertical elements; M–P for cap elements; Q–U for horizontal elements; V for voussoirs; W–Z for frames) in what seemed endless rows—a formidable library of Roman marble ornament. Following the Jacobs catalogue, design researchers and field workers could identify each piece in the "bone yard," and, based on its findspot and quadrant, estimate its original position vis-à-vis the main walls of the Marble Court.

Page 30, illustrated here, shows at the top three different sketches of the apex of the pediment, identified as the "Pediment Peak," numbered 61.143 (the 143rd piece found in 1961), and coded S3R/4 (obviously, a pediment apex was considered a horizontal element). It was found at coordinates East 22 and North 58.5, in quadrant S-NW, number 4, at elevation 97.60. In order to provide more information, a simple vertical section and a top view of the block, each with copious dimensions, were also sketched in addition to the standard three-quarter view. Construction and design features, such as the lewis hole for lifting at the top of the pediment, or setting lines and breaks that could aid the matching of two pieces and hence the reconstruction, are carefully included—for instance, the flat area on the apex indicates that the pediment was surmounted by an acroterion. The comment on the right margin "Raking ∟ approx. 22.5°?" turns out to be an excellent field measurement: the correct raking angle of the pediment is 37/100, or 22°.

The piece sketched at the bottom of the page is the upside-down view of the north corner cornice of the pediment joining the second-story entablature. Its peculiar projecting end that is approximately four to five centimeters deep (shown as a separate, right-side up, simple elevation on the facing page) illustrates a unique detail that helped us to solve the particularly difficult design problem of determining which story the pediment belonged to. FKY

1. Hanfmann 1972, 97.
2. Hanfmann 1972, 81.

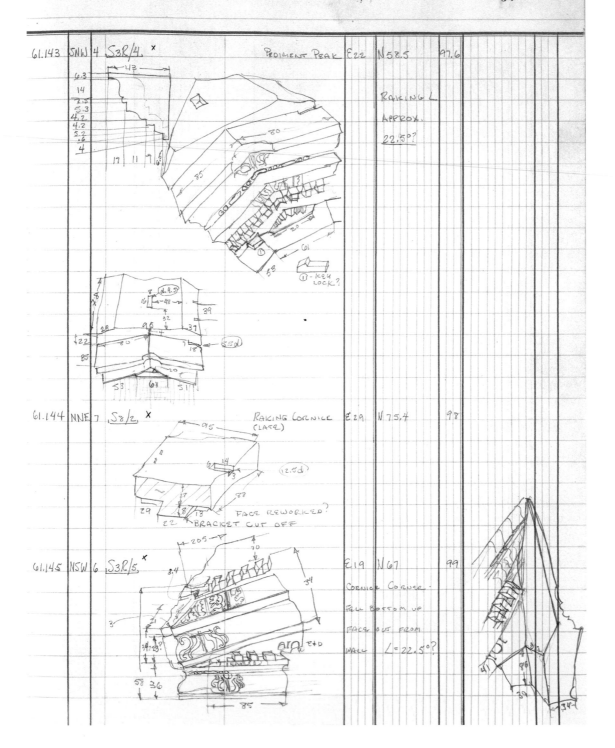

61.143 SNW 4 S3R/4 ✗   PEDIMENT PEAK E22 N58.5 97.6

RAKING ∠
APPROX.
22.5°?

61.144 NNE 1 S8/2 ✗   RAKING CORNICE E.29 N75.4 9.8
(LATE)

FACE REWORKED?
BRACKET CUT OFF

61.145 NSW 6 S3R/5 ✗   E.19 N67 99
CORNICE CORNER.
FELL BOTTOM UP
FACE OUT FROM
WALL ∠ = 22.5°?

MARBLE COURT: PRELIMINARY DESIGN
SKETCHES 2 AND 3

Fikret K. Yegül, 1965

Blueprint copy on wove paper of felt-tip pen used in
watercolor or wash style on yellow tracing paper

21.1 × 29 cm (8¼ × 11⅜ in.) and 21.4 × 29 cm
(8⅜ × 11⅜ in.)

Archaeological Exploration of Sardis

These two studies are among numerous
"idea sketches" prepared in an attempt to
understand the arrangement of the aedicular facades of the Marble Court, a ceremonial space opening off the palaestra of the
Roman Bath-Gymnasium Complex, and
probably dedicated to the imperial cult.
An inscription carved on the first-story architrave dedicating this space to the Emperors Caracalla and Geta (name erased),
their mother Julia Domna, the entire house
of the Augusti, and the Roman Senate and
People, helped date the original construction to about 210–211. From 1960 to
1963 some eight hundred marble blocks,
representing an astounding variety of architectural ornament, were sketched, cata-
logued, photographed, and moved out of
the Court (see cat. 35). The decision to reconstruct, from the ground up, the rich,
columnar structure in the so-called Severan Baroque style of Asia Minor, was
bold and challenging. Actual work on the
design and reconstruction of the Court
was started in 1964 and 1965 by joining
matching blocks to sketches made in the
field during the previous years and creating field mock-ups. Between 1964 and its
completion in 1971, the Marble Court was
an all-consuming project for those involved in its design and actual reconstruction.

These two sketches, both done in 1965,
show two solutions with small variations
in the order and sequence of the two-
storied columnar aediculae. Both retain on
the first story a central, arcuated pediment
("Syrian pediment") carried by four monumental, spirally fluted columns in im-
ported giallo antico marble. The first-story
columns raised on a continuous podium,

with L-shaped corner entablatures, are
also common to both schemes. The main
difference is in the arrangement of the second story: in sketch 2 (36A) the ends of
the pediment support one of the two
columns of flanking upper-story aediculae;
in sketch 3 (36B) both columns of the
upper-story aediculae (of unequal height)
rest on the raking cornice of the pediment.
The sketches also show variations in the
sequence and design of the second-story
aediculae and their entablatures, both of
which display awkward inside corners.
Neither of these improbable arrangements
proved right, and apparently there are no
precedents in classical architecture for the
placement of columns directly on a raking
cornice. However, as aptly observed by
George Hanfmann, who commented in his
July 1966 *Newsletter* from Sardis that
"Fikret Yegül has begun to wrestle with
various problems of design,"[1] these
sketches reflect the continuing search and
struggle of an architecture student, then
barely tutored in his classical orders, who,
along with others entrusted with various
aspects of this project, was learning on
the job.

Documents of our growing knowledge
about the puzzling structure, these drawings, along with a number of other hard-
line study perspectives and elevations (see
cats. 37, 38), illustrated many an evening's
"Marble Court design conference" at
Sardis, and sparked heated discussions
presided over by Hanfmann and Henry
Detweiler, the Expedition director and associate director, and James Yarnell, a civil
engineer from Cornell.

The problem was with the position of
the so-called pedimented gate (the arcuated pediment originally crowned not a
gate but an apse that probably housed an
altar, and the apse was cut through to
form a "gate" only in the early fourth
century). So obsessed were we with the
idea of a "gate" that we did not see that
placing the arcuated pediment on the
second story would avoid the unhappy
arrangement of columnar aediculae resting
directly on the pediment, and the improb-
ably forced placement of the heavier

straight entablature (composed of three
pieces) on the second story instead of the
first, where it logically and traditionally
belonged.

In the end, enlightenment came not at
the drafting board, nor at the long evening
conferences, but in the field, when in the
spring of 1967 Mehmet Cemal Bolgil, the
supervising architect of the Marble Court
reconstruction, using original mason's
markings that firmly matched together certain architectural pieces (and other field
criteria), placed the pediment on the second story, and reversed the first and
second story entablatures—then every-
thing about the design fell into place. The
pediment became the crowning element of
a magnificent double-story, eight-column
central ensemble, which has precedents in
Roman imperial architecture. The correct,
final scheme is represented in a perspective
made in 1968 by David De Long (cat. 38).
FKY

1. Hanfmann 1972, 182.

SKETCH ②

SKETCH ③

37

MARBLE COURT: RECONSTRUCTED WEST ELEVATION, 1:50

Fikret K. Yegül, 1966

Black ink and graphite on translucent vellum paper

66.5 × 109.3 cm (26½ × 43 in.)

Archaeological Exploration of Sardis, MC-66.12

This is one of the attempts on paper to restore the complicated aedicular sequence of the first and the second orders of the west facade of the Marble Court, described by Hanfmann in 1966 as "tentative." He further elaborated, justly, that the Marble Court reconstruction effort was "perhaps the largest undertaking of this sort north of Baalbek, and will be a splendid memorial to our efforts when it gets done—but it will take some doing."[1] This hard-line elevation drawn to scale is based on the preceding freehand sketches, but it is closer to the 1965 perspective sketch 3 (cat. 36B) with its pair of aediculae fully resting on the raking cornice of the pediment. The lower story retains the L-shaped aediculae seen in all previous proposals while the upper story has single-column corner aediculae, representing a more felicitous and classically correct solution—though, here, it was placed on the wrong level. The drawing indicates that by the summer of 1966, I was able to match correctly the corner entablatures of the first and second story orders; however, I was still struggling ("wrestling" Hanfmann had said) to assign the lighter, two-piece entablature (the order of the pediment) on the first story and the heavier, three-piece entablature (which properly belonged to the lower story, of course) on the second story because of ignorance or an inability to visualize the pediment as the crowning, upper level element of a double-tiered, eight-column central ensemble. FKY

1. Hanfmann 1972, 196 and 198; fig. 150 shows an almost identical version of our illustration.

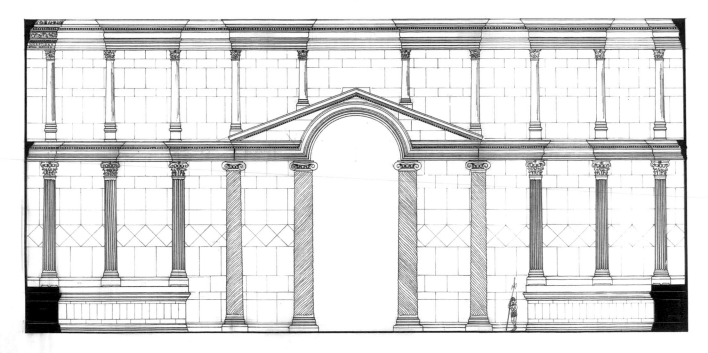

M.C. 66.12
WEST WALL ELEVATION .I.   1/50   fky

38

MARBLE COURT: RECONSTRUCTED VIEW LOOKING WEST

David G. De Long, 1968

Black ink with traces of graphite on translucent vellum paper

66.1 × 87.3 cm (26 × 34½ in)

Archaeological Exploration of Sardis, MC-68.14

Published in Yegül 1986, fig. 92.

This 1968 perspective by David De Long, based on earlier studies (cats. 36 and 37, among others), represents the final, and what we believe to be the correct, design for the restoration of the Marble Court. The main architectural problem was solved in the field in 1967 when the arcuated pediment was placed on the second story. The raking cornice received its proper end and apex acroteria (instead of the awkward columns), and a small, conjectural apse was introduced on the second story, directly below the arch, ostensibly to house an imperial statue. The scheme represented in De Long's perspective is the one reconstructed in the field and represents the latest phase of the Court, where the original apse on the ground story was later cut through to create a direct passage into the *frigidarium* of the Bath-Gymnasium, and the pedimented ensemble became an imposing, double-storied actual gateway, instead of the visual and symbolic focus of the imperial cult. The "pedimented gate" is supported by two tiers of spirally fluted giallo antico columns (second-story columns are shown as plain shafts in the perspective); the monumental first story has Ionic capitals; the second story, under the pediment, has acanthus-and-fluting capitals ("Pergamene"). First-story aedicula columns, also of giallo antico, carry Composite capitals; those of the second story, with plain white marble shafts, have Corinthian capitals.

With its columnar aediculae alternating in shape and position (those of the second story are not placed directly over those of the first but rather over the void between them), enclosing a monumental space on three sides and closed off on the fourth, or the palaestra, side, by a double-storied columnar screen (not shown in the drawing), the Marble Court of Sardis is one of the most complex and sumptuous examples of this kind of ornamental marble facade (fig. 27). Dubbed "Asiatic facades" (because of their popularity in Asia Minor), they became the hallmark of the architecture of the Late Empire, adorning stage fronts (*scaenae frons*), city gates, fountain structures, and, as in our example, ceremonial halls in the context of Roman bath-gymnasia in Asia Minor.
FKY

Fig. 27. Marble Court, after reconstruction, looking west (1972).

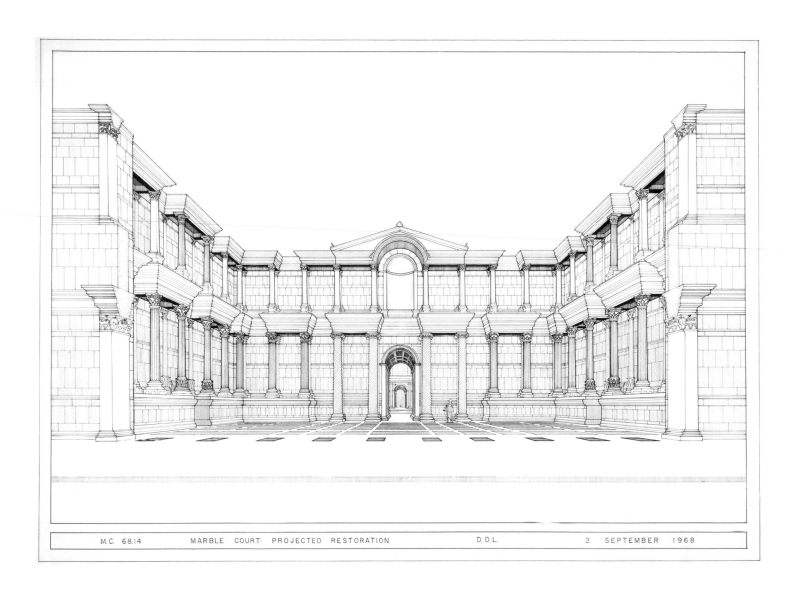

M.C. 68.14 MARBLE COURT PROJECTED RESTORATION D.D.L. 2 SEPTEMBER 1968

39

LATE ROMAN SYNAGOGUE: RECON-
STRUCTED WITH ADJACENT PORTICO
TO THE EAST AND BYZANTINE SHOPS
AND PORTICO TO THE SOUTH, THREE-
DIMENSIONAL MODEL, 1:80

Constructed under the direction of Andrew Seager,
1995–96

Basswood, plaster of paris, clay, photographic paper

Base, 61 × 131.9 cm (24 × 51¹⁵/₁₆ in.)

Yeshiva University Museum

Published in a text citation in Fine 1996,
159–60 no. 20.

The Synagogue at Sardis, created perhaps as early as the fourth century A.D. and continuing in use as late as the seventh century, is the largest synagogue known from antiquity. Sardis probably had a Jewish community in the third century B.C., when Jews were settled in western Anatolia by the Seleucid king (of Syria, Palestine, and other Near Eastern lands) Antiochus III, according to Jewish historian Josephus;[1] and perhaps much earlier, in the sixth century B.C., if Sardis is Sepharad, a location of Jewish exiles mentioned in the Bible (Obadiah 20). By the middle of the first century B.C., the Jewish community at Sardis enjoyed privileges with respect to meetings and meeting places, worship, adjudication of internal disputes, and special food.[2] Specific evidence for the Jewish community apart from the Synagogue consists of epigraphical texts and iconographic images of the Late Roman era.

The Synagogue was identified as such from its contents of votive menorahs, reference to the dedication of a seven-branched candlestick in a Greek inscription, and short inscriptions in Hebrew.[3] It occupied one wing of the Roman Bath-Gymnasium Complex (figs. 2, 24, 28). The building wing originally had been subdivided into three halls, of unknown function; it was remodeled for use as a synagogue in the fourth or fifth century A.D. The entrance was located at the east end and led to a forecourt, the open court of which featured a central fountain and was surrounded by a colonnaded portico. Three doorways led from the forecourt to the main hall. Against the wall separating them, and between the central and side doorways, were two pavilions (one of which may have held the Torah). At its far (west) end, the hall terminated in a semicircular apse, which contained tiers of seats, presumably for elders of the community. Freestanding piers supported a clerestory, or raised section above the central nave, to allow illumination of the interior (from windows in the raised section). In the model, part of the roof over the central nave of the main hall has been omitted to reveal the construction and decoration of the interior.

The model was made for the exhibition *Sacred Realm: The Emergence of the Synagogue in the Ancient World,* held at Yeshiva University in 1996.[4] CHG

1. Josephus, *Jewish Antiquities* 12.147–53.
2. Josephus, *Jewish Antiquities* 14.235, 259–61.
3. Kroll 2001, 42; Cross 2002.
4. Fine 1996.

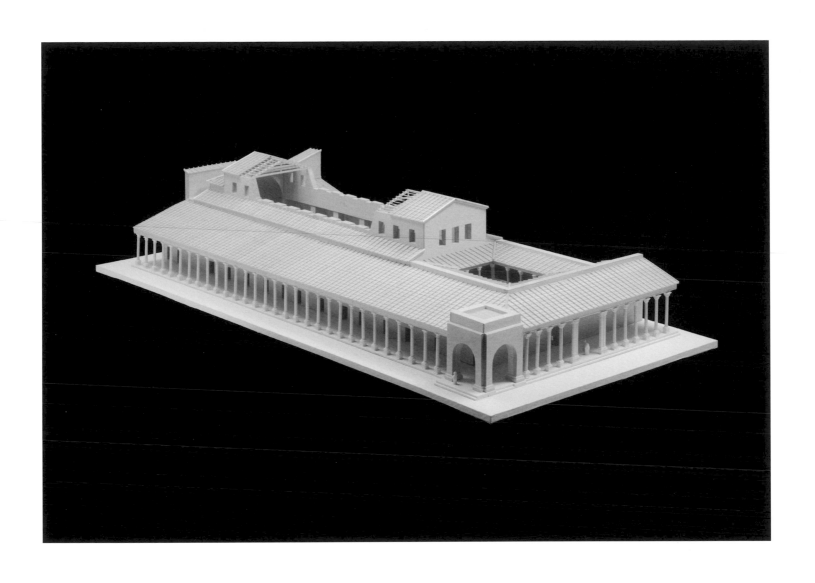

40

Late Roman Synagogue: Reconstructed View of the East End of the Main Hall, Looking East

James Anderson, 1976; Andrew R. Seager, 1996

Photocopy of original drawing in ink on Mylar

91.7 × 60.5 cm (36 × 23¾ in.)

Archaeological Exploration of Sardis, SYN-1841.76A

A segment of the north wall, which had fallen "without breaking apart," contributed evidence for the original height of the outer walls.[1] The drawing was made to show the clerestory arrangement of the ceiling and the massive piers, as well as the pavilion-like shrines, which flank the central entrance from the forecourt, and the decoration of colored marble revetment (*opus sectile*).   CHG

1. Seager 1972, 427; Hanfmann 1966, 52.

41

SYNAGOGUE: PLAN, WITH RECONSTRUCTED FLOOR MOSAIC

Lawrence J. Majewski and Hüseyin Özlü, 1966–71

Photomontage of ink drawings with added ink

38.2 × 124 cm (15 × 48¾ in.)

Archaeological Exploration of Sardis, SYN-1351.68

This drawing presents an overview of floor mosaic designs and their arrangement in the Synagogue and in the segment of sidewalk portico immediately in front of the building. It shows a series of rectangular "panels" or "panels within panels" arranged in file along the sidewalk portico, around the portico of the forecourt and down the central nave of the main hall, and individually in the bays (between piers) of the main hall. (Similar organization and designs characterize floor mosaics in sidewalk porticos outside the Byzantine Shops and on the other side of the street from the Shops; see cats. 12, 13). The mosaics are made of cut cubes (tesserae) of naturally colored stone and terracotta; their colors are pale blue gray, dark blue black, yellow, lavender, white (all stone), and red brown (terracotta). To the modern eye, the panel series and geometric decoration of the floor mosaics recall carpet assemblages, like those one sees today in mosques. The medium and the rough square form of the tesserae, however, give mosaics a textural quality all their own (which the linear style of the drawings does not convey). Most ancient mosaics probably were not meant to imitate textiles; they had a separate tradition.

Few of the panels have survived complete (cf. fig. 28), but their geometric design permits full reconstruction. Some panels were reconstructed partly from photographs, the mosaics having been drawn, at a scale of 1:20, in pencil by Majewski, then traced in ink by Özlü (a grade school teacher from the nearby village of Durasıllı).

Between 1966 and 1973, all the Synagogue mosaics (1200 square meters, or 12,915 square feet) were lifted and backed with steel-reinforced concrete; and all were replaced in their original locations except for the apse mosaic and the panel-center compositions that contain inscriptions (in Greek), which were transported to the Archaeological and Ethnographical Museum in Manisa.[1]   CHG

1. Hanfmann 1983, 174 and fig. 28; Kroll 2001.

Fig. 28. Synagogue, after reconstruction (1989).

North of the Synagogue is the south side of the palaestra of the Late Roman Bath-Gymnasium Complex; south of the Synagogue are some of the Byzantine Shops.

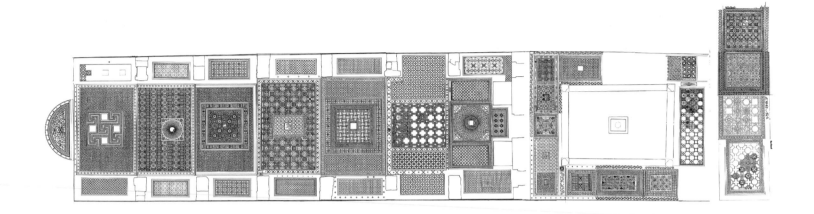

42

SECTOR PN: BYZANTINE CHURCH E,
RECONSTRUCTED NORTH ELEVATION

Hans H. Buchwald, c. 1984

Black ink on Mylar

29.4 × 43.3 cm (11⅝ × 17 in.)

Archaeological Exploration of Sardis, PN-163

One of the latest major buildings known at Sardis is a small Byzantine church of the thirteenth century (fig. 29), Church E. It was built during the half-century of Byzantine government "exile" in Magnesia ad Sipylum (present-day Manisa) and Nymphaeum (present-day Kemalpaşa)—both approximately sixty kilometers (about forty mi.) east of Sardis—when Constantinople, captured in the Fourth Crusade, was the capital of a Latin Empire (A.D. 1204–61). With its modest size, multiple domes, multiplane facades, and rich decoration in stone and brick, Church E had the jewel-like quality of similar, somewhat later churches that survive intact (for example, the Churches of the Holy Apostles in Thessaloniki and of the Pantanassa in Mistra).

Church E was excavated in 1962, 1963, 1972, 1973, and 2000. It had been built over the ruins of an Early Christian basilica, Church EA—excavated in 1962, 1972, 1973, and 1984—which was first recognized as an earlier basilica in 1972. CHG

Fig. 29. Byzantine Church E, surviving ruins of the church, looking west (1973).

The outer apse partially visible in the foreground belongs to Church EA, the Early Christian predecessor of Church E, which was built over the remains of the earlier building.

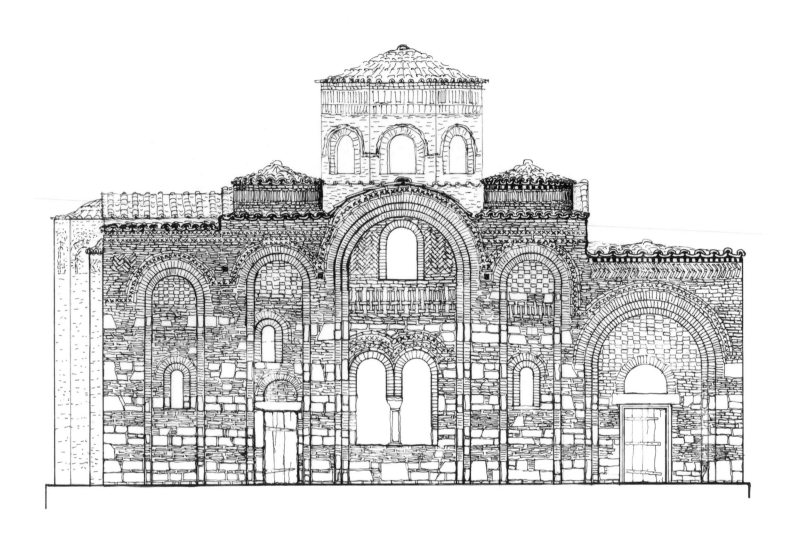

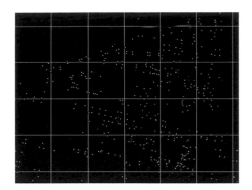  

Fig. 30. Left to right: a "point cloud" shown on the computer screen; points connected with lines to form Roman features excavated in complex of Late Roman houses; surfaces formed from wire-frame model.

Philip T. Stinson, 2003, computer-generated drawing. Archaeological Exploration of Sardis, M-141.

Infinite Points

Nicholas D. Cahill and Philip T. Stinson

"Infinite Points" is a metaphor for the new electronic and computerized technologies that are dramatically changing the way graphic recording is done at Sardis and opening a window onto its complex urban history. Computer drawings differ from conventional drawings by hand in a number of important respects. First, they may be three-dimensional, and so record information which is not innately included in a drawing on flat paper or Mylar (e.g., cats. 47–50). Computer files are easily modified, updated, and expanded to incorporate the results of new research, while a conventional drawing is limited by the size of the original sheet and can be erased and redrawn only a certain number of times. Digital drawings are independent of scale: whereas pen-and-ink drawings are made at specific scales, some to show more detail of smaller areas, others to show wider areas but with less resolution, a single digital drawing can record objects as small as individual potsherds and still cover the entire region of Lydia. Like Jorge Luis Borges's perfect map which, however, could never be unfolded because it would completely cover the territory it was supposed to represent,[1] the digital maps are virtually at a scale of 1:1. Finally, a digital drawing can incorporate more information about what is being drawn than can a pencil or ink drawing. It may include a more complex set of conventions, not simply line weights, dashes, and dots, and the other conventions in black and white, but also colors, textures, opacities, and so on. It may be organized into layers that separate elements of different types. To include more information about the objects being drawn, elements of a digital drawing can also be linked to a database that may be searched and analyzed (a Geographic Information System or GIS). The drawing thus becomes much more than a graphic recording of features: it becomes a tool for analysis (cat. 48).

The most straightforward application of digital technologies to graphic recording involves electronic surveying and computer-aided drawing (CAD). The electronic transit or total station uses infrared light and reflecting prisms to measure angles and distances much more accurately and over longer distances than the alidade and plane table (cat. 9A) or other traditional surveying instruments (fig. 21). Computer surveying does not replace field sheets in pencil and inked drawings on Mylar, but it does provide a much better foundation on which to build those drawings. In the 1990s the electronic total station became the standard method of surveying at Sardis, replacing the alidade and plane table.

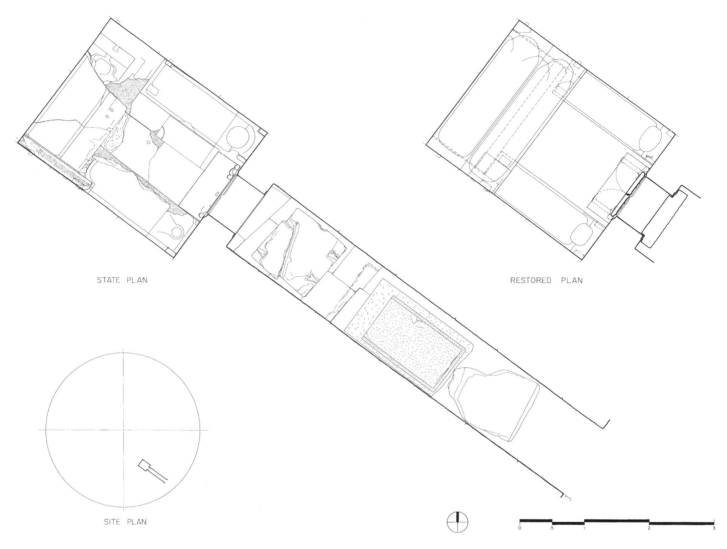

STATE PLAN

RESTORED PLAN

SITE PLAN

Fig. 31. State plan of tomb chamber at Lale Tepe, Ahmetli.

Philip T. Stinson, 1999, 2001, black ink with traces of graphite on Mylar. Archaeological Exploration of Sardis, T-59.

The tomb consists of a masonry interment chamber and a long entranceway or *dromos*, all covered by an artificial mound about 50 meters in diameter.

Experiments with three-dimensional computer modeling techniques are in the fledgling stage at Sardis, but have already proved tremendously useful in visualizing and mapping the ancient city and its monuments. Three-dimensional computer models have been made to reconstruct the complex architectural history of the Lydian city wall, to illustrate the phasing of Late Roman houses, to study the modern and ancient terrain of the site, and to record a painted Lydian tomb, among other projects. The creation of a digital model begins by taking many measurements. A two-person team using a total station can take up to five hundred measurements in a day; with a Global Positioning System (GPS) receiver a single person can take many thousands of points. The total station is normally used for precise architectural recording, while a GPS is more serviceable for topographical features. Field measurements taken with either system are downloaded automatically into CAD or GIS software. Each measurement is represented on the computer screen as a single point in a simulation of its three-dimensional location in space. Then the points can be connected together with lines; many associated lines form shapes that resemble the physical forms from which they

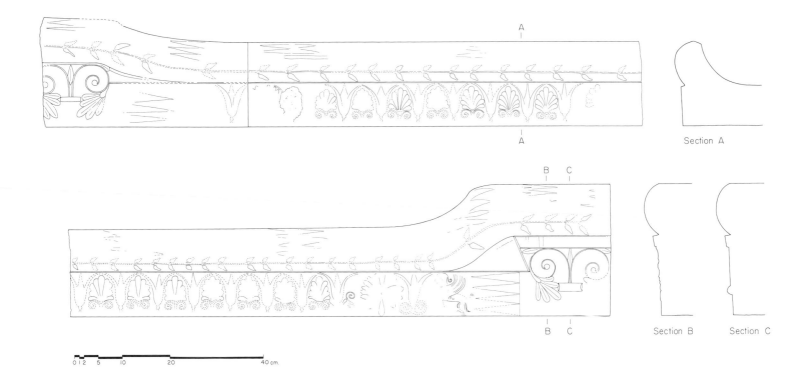

Section A

Section B   Section C

0 1 2 5   10   20   40 cm.

Fig. 32. Lale Tepe, Ahmetli, elevation and sections of double *kline*, detail of painted frieze on front of double *kline*.

Catherine S. Alexander, 1999, 2002, black ink with traces of graphite on Mylar. Archaeological Exploration of Sardis, T-66.

The most elaborate surviving carved and painted decoration in the tomb is on the long, rounded mattress edge and bed frame of the double *kline* facing the front of the tomb. A painted frieze of red, green, and black palmettes alternating with red and green lotus flowers dominates the flat horizontal length. The design

changes in the center, but cannot be identified. On both ends of this frieze, hints of a red and black rosette and a red, black, and green sphinx in profile survive. A straight green vine with paired leaves runs the length of the curved mattress edge above, and the top of this edge features a green and red zigzag pattern. This zigzag pattern may have alternating stripes, as seen on *klinai* in Greek vase painting. The voluted designs at each end of the *kline* that resemble Aeolic-style capitals are carved in shallow relief and painted. As the drawing indicates, the left capital was trimmed in antiquity, presumably because the block was mistakenly made too long.

were originally derived: walls, a topographic surface, or other features (fig. 30). These shapes can then be "textured" by applying digital images as a sort of wallpaper (cats. 49, 50).

One such computer model created recently applies this new technology in the recording and study of a Late Archaic painted tomb known as Lale Tepe (cat. 50). The model was made using "texture-mapping" techniques. Texture mapping is the method of placing digital photographs into a simulation of their actual three-dimensional or spatial context. This involved taking many digital photographs of

the wall, ceiling, and floor surfaces. Using the dimensions of the tomb chamber and model-making software, a three-dimensional "wire frame" of the tomb chamber was made. Then the digital photographs were texture-mapped onto the surfaces of the wire-frame model like a skin over a framework, to recreate the tomb chamber in digital form at almost a one-to-one scale, or one pixel (the smallest dot on a computer screen) to one millimeter. The model also reconstructs the burial couches (*klinai*) that were broken by tomb robbers, their painted decorations, and the wall paintings of the back walls and the ceiling. The computer model will

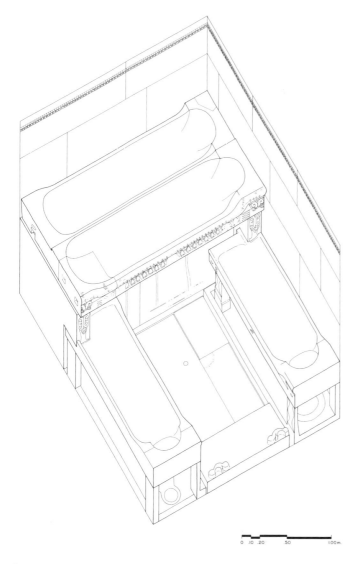

Fig. 33. Axonometric reconstruction drawing of the tomb chamber at Lale Tepe.

Catherine S. Alexander, 2001, 2003, black ink with traces of graphite on Mylar. Archaeological Exploration of Sardis, T-74.

The tomb chamber provided for seven interments on two levels. In the limestone floor are three hollows for the deceased, two along the sides and one at the back; three marble *klinai* were installed directly above them, the one at the back a double *kline*. Marble *orthostates* supported the ends of the double *kline*. An additional upright limestone slab filled in the opening underneath the length of the double *kline* and obscured the back floor bed from view. The marble *orthostates* at the head and foot of the double *kline* feature projections that fit into shallow depressions carved into the tops of the two marble *klinai* on the right and left sides of the chamber. Six of the eight legs supporting the two single *klinai* on either side of the chamber were carved from the limestone blocks of the chamber walls. This and other evidence indicate that all seven *klinai* and floor beds are part of the original design of the tomb.

serve alongside traditional drawings—before it was made, the whole tomb was recorded with traditional drawings and photographs; the ink-line plans, sections, and details drawn on Mylar are very useful (figs. 31–33). The computer model, however, provides a more comprehensive record of the painted decoration on the walls and ceiling. Drawings and photographs are usually done only of the most significant features, and by their nature must be selective. Because a computer model is fully three-dimensional and inclusive, it calls attention to difficult archaeological problems such as the lack of physical evidence, and to the methodologies used to resolve those questions. With traditional methods of orthogonal or perspective drawing, one is naturally inclined to focus on areas where the evidence is better preserved, or ignore areas where evidence is lacking.

The benefits of computer technologies were initially expected at the practical level of more exact surveying. It was difficult to predict, however, the fruits of applying these techniques to the topography of the city site. The rough and varied landscape of Sardis (fig. 3) has always impeded surveying and accurate recording of topographical features, and thus our understanding of the site as a whole. Maps of Sardis created by the Butler Expedition and by architects and surveyors at Sardis in the 1960s were important tools for the study of the site and are testaments to the skills of the surveyors and architects who drew them. They were limited, however, by the available technologies and media. For example, with paper or Mylar drawings there is a trade-off between scale and extent: a map covering a wide area, such as Butler's larger plan (see cat. 43), can show a wide area but with limited detail, while maps at a larger scale, such as Butler's smaller map or the Master Urban Plan (cats. 43, 44), can show more detail, but are restricted in extent. New digital maps of Sardis record its complex topography at a very fine resolution over a wide area, are simple to update, and can easily be modified to show or accentuate different features (cat. 46). By making the digital map in three dimensions, moreover, one can indicate topography in different ways and the map can become a tool for further topographical analysis. Contour lines have become a conventional means of representing three-dimensional relief in two dimensions, but they are by no means the best or the only way to do so. With digital maps, one can recreate the ground surface in the computer: as a grid of evenly spaced points (a Digital Elevation Model, or DEM, such as cat. 47) or as a series of triangles or other shapes that approximate the ground surface (such as a Triangulated Irregular Network, or TIN). The surface model can be used for further topographic research: to study, for example, drainage, erosion, and other processes that change the landscape, and so study what the terrain might have looked like in antiquity. It may also be used to create maps and views of the site that are more easily understood—oblique views or shaded maps (cats. 47, 49). Such images not only give a dramatic view of the landscape and vegetation of Lydia but also help us investigate the relations between human habitation and the natural landscape in antiquity.

1. Borges and Bioy Casares 1971, 123.

43

"MAP OF THE RUINS OF SARDIS,"
1:8000 REDUCED IN PUBLICATION TO
1:16,000

Lloyd T. Emory, 1913

Black ink with traces of graphite on wove paper

44.2 × 34.6 cm (17 7/16 × 13 9/16 in.)

Department of Art and Archaeology, Princeton
University

Published in Butler 1922, ill. 18; Vann 1989, fig. 9.

This is one of two maps of the site prepared by the Butler Expedition. Like
Giovanni Battista Borra in his map of
about 1750 (cat. 3), Butler's surveyor
Lloyd Emory chose to orient his map with
south at the top. The orientation is not to
true or magnetic north, however, but is
fitted to the natural topography, with the
Pactolus Stream running along the right
side of the map and the railroad horizon-
tally across the bottom. This was apparently a matter of convenience in laying out
the sheet rather than a deliberate carto-
graphic decision.

Emory's map covers an area of about
7.9 square kilometers (1943 acres). He
recorded the topography of the site with
contour lines spaced at twenty-five-meter
intervals, adding hatching to indicate the
steep cliffs of the Acropolis. While contour
lines do not give an impression of the relief
as immediate and intuitive as Borra's brush
strokes do, they are crisper and more ob-
jective. They enable the reader to measure
the elevation of points on the map, since
the lines are labeled with their elevations
above sea level. Emory used stippling to
indicate the floodplain of the Pactolus and
included both modern and ancient buildings. The drawing of the surviving Roman
buildings at Sardis is fuller and more accurate than Borra's, indicating more of the
Roman city wall and additional buildings,
and recording the alignments of the
Roman buildings more accurately. He used
dashed lines to reconstruct the course of
features such as the Roman city wall. Features are more accurately plotted—
understandably, given the much longer
time that Emory had to work at Sardis.

The orientation of the Byzantine walls on
the southwest part of the Acropolis (labeled "Wall" on "Akropolis"), for instance, is quite accurate on Emory's map,
while Borra's drawing shows them on the
northeast side of the hill (E in cat. 3).
Emory did not, however, indicate some details that Borra included, such as the
stadium vaults.

The letters assigned to buildings—A, B,
C, etc.—are still used by the current Sardis
Expedition: Building B, for instance, is the
Bath-Gymnasium Complex (cats. 35–38).

Emory drew a larger foldout map, not
included in this exhibition, that was intended to cover some 37 square kilometers
(9200 acres). This map showed not only
the city proper but also the cemeteries,
which were an important part of Butler's
research; the aqueduct leading from the
Acropolis into the Tmolus Range; and the
foothills of the Tmolus. The map is
unfinished, with only about 19 square
kilometers (4700 acres) actually mapped.
Butler intended to complete the survey and
draw the ancient remains in more detail,
but World War I and then his untimely
death in 1922 prevented him from com-
pleting the project.   NDC

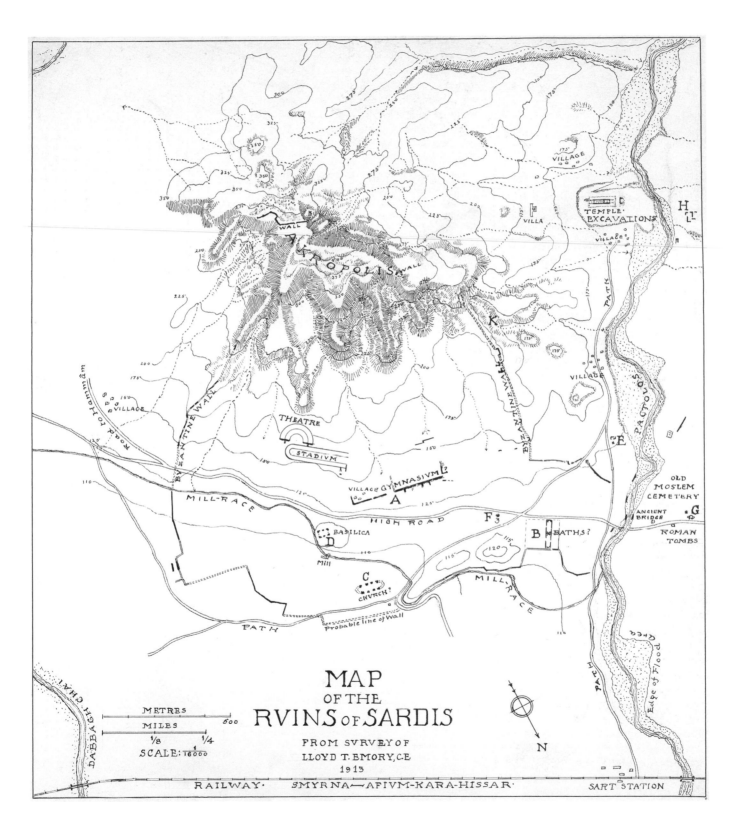

MAP
OF THE
RVINS OF SARDIS

FROM SVRVEY OF
LLOYD T. EMORY, C.E.
1913

44

Sardis Master Urban Plan, 1:2000

Crawford H. Greenewalt, Jr., Robert L. Vann, John L. Miller, Fikret K. Yegül, Stuart L. Carter, 1974; Kathryn L. Gleason, Thomas N. Howe, 1981; Timothy R. Barner, 1986; Philip T. Stinson, 1993, 1995

Black ink and graphite on Mylar

150.5 × 106.7 cm (59¼ × 42 in.)

Archaeological Exploration of Sardis, M26U-101

Published frequently.

In 1962, to meet the needs of the recently resumed excavations, a base map of Sardis at a scale of 1:2000 was prepared for the Expedition by the Turkish State Board of Waterworks (Devlet Su Işleri) in the nearby town of Salihli. The Master Urban Plan is a 1974 update based on the 1962 survey and subsequent excavation. The scale is four times larger than Butler's map, so it shows finer details of topography and architecture. For instance, the base map showed elevation with contour lines at five-meter intervals, rather than at twenty-five, so that details of the topography stand out more clearly. It does not cover as wide an area as either of Butler's maps, however. It maps some 3.80 square kilometers (939 acres), half the area of Butler's small map and only one-tenth as much as Butler's larger map. As excavation proceeded, architects added ancient buildings and other features to the topographic framework, creating an evolving record of the site and its ancient remains.

The Master Urban Plan introduces a feature not found on previous maps of Sardis: a coordinate system or grid covering the entire site. This allows the locations of buildings and artifacts to be recorded, satisfying one of the primary goals of a map. The grid on the Master Urban Plan is called the "B-grid" since it is based on Building B, the Roman Bath-Gymnasium Complex. This grid was developed in the first year of the Harvard-Cornell excavation; Building B was chosen as a reference because it is a prominent, permanent feature of the landscape and was convenient to the parts of the site being excavated. It is a purely local grid, however, not used outside the excavations at Sardis, so features recorded in the B-grid cannot be located in other coordinate systems (such as latitude and longitude). In the early years problems arose in surveying and extending the grid over the entire site with the required accuracy. Independent grids were therefore established for excavations in the Artemis Temple, in Building CG at the east edge of the city, and on the Acropolis. Recent excavations have used the B-grid exclusively.

The ragged, rugged look of the map results from some thirty years of use, correction, and modification, and countless rollings and unrollings during travel to and from Turkey. Places where the tooth of the Mylar has worn through result from the erasing of ink multiple times. Many hands have worked on this drawing, as the list of initials and years indicates. This map—although not as conventionally consistent or beautiful as some of the other maps and drawings in the exhibition—acquired a high use value over the years, and even though digital drawings have replaced it, the Sardis Expedition continues to bring it to the site each summer.
NDC, PTS

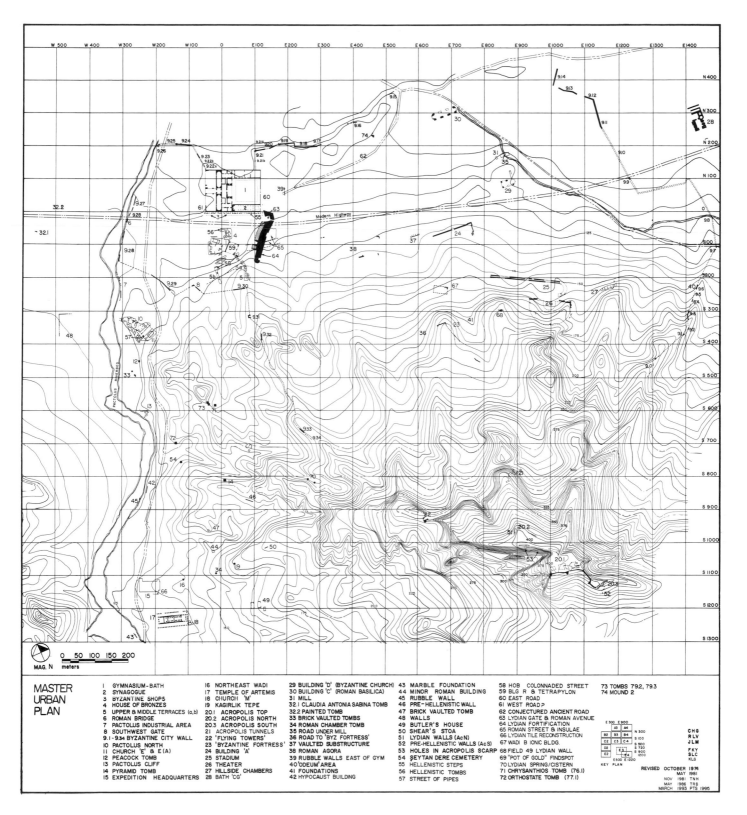

45

MAP 37, ONE OF 47 TOPOGRAPHIC
SURVEY MAPS OF THE SARDIS REGION

Turkish General Directorate of Maps, 1981–85

Colored ink on Mylar

100.1 × 70.1 cm (39½ × 27⅝ in.)

Turkish General Directorate of Maps

While the Master Urban Plan provided an adequate map of the city of Sardis, it is too limited in extent for many aspects of the Expedition's current research. In 1981, at the Expedition's request, the Turkish General Directorate of Maps began to make a series of forty-seven maps at the same scale as the 1962 map (1:2000). When finished in 1985, the maps covered two major areas: the region from the Acropolis and Necropolis hills south into the foothills of the Tmolus—roughly the same region as Butler's map—and Bin Tepe, the cemetery of tumuli about eleven kilometers (seven mi.) north of the site (fig. 34). The forty-seven individual sheets cover an area of 108 square kilometers (26,687 acres), twenty-eight times as large as the Master Urban Plan (cat. 44). Topography is recorded in two-meter contour intervals, with intermediate contour lines at one-meter intervals where appropriate, giving much finer definition to the terrain than any previous site map. In addition to topography, these maps record modern buildings, roads and tracks, field boundaries, permanent and seasonal streams, vegetation, and other features. The maps are thus both more detailed and more extensive than any previous map.

The map included here covers the Acropolis of Sardis, whose top is near the center of the map (compare the Sardis Urban Plan derived from these maps, cat. 46). The former Izmir-Ankara highway crosses the upper right corner of the map. Contour lines are shown in brown, streams in blue, different sorts of vegetation with green symbols. Modern field boundaries, drawn in black, often follow the lines of buried ancient roads, terraces, and other features.

Like the Master Urban Plan, the Turkish maps indicate their coordinate system, using numbers around the sides of the sheets and grid ticks at 200-meter intervals. Unlike the Master Urban Plan, however, they are oriented to true north, and use a worldwide coordinate system rather than one purely local to the site: the Universal Transverse Mercator (UTM) projection. UTM is a common projection, or method of mapping the spherical earth onto a flat surface. Distortion caused by the curvature of the earth is not a problem over the short distances that previous maps of Sardis had covered; over longer distances, however, even as short as the distance from Sardis to Bin Tepe, the curvature of the earth must be considered in drawing a map. Because they are given in a standard coordinate system, features on these maps can therefore be related to locations anywhere in the world.   NDC

Fig. 34. Key plan for Turkish topographic maps, showing map 37 highlighted.

Nicholas D. Cahill, 2003. Archaeological Exploration of Sardis, M-138.